The Autism Journey: A Parent's Guide

Empowering Your Child Toward Success One Step at a Time

The Autism Journey: A Parent's Guide

Empowering Your Child Toward Success One Step at a Time

Emmaline MacBeath, M.Ed, M.S.M
with Cameron O'Hair
Illustrated by Ryan Winters

The Autism Journey: A Parent's Guide
Empowering Your Child Toward Success One Step at a Time

Copyright © 2018 by Emmaline MacBeath
Illustrations Copyright © 2018 by Ryan Winters

All rights reserved. No part of this publication may be reproduced, translated, stored in a retrieval system, or transmitted, in any form or by any means, electronic, mechanical, photocopying, microfilming, recording, or otherwise, without prior written permission from the publisher.

This book is intended as a resource on autism and to point the reader to the source materials that contain a more thorough overview of the subject. None of the information presented in this book is meant to be a prescription for any kind of treatment. Reference to other organizations and materials is for convenience only and is not intended as an endorsement.

No therapy should be initiated unless recommended and supervised by a qualified professional. Every child is different and requires an individualized treatment plan as created by the parent or guardian and qualified professionals. These professionals and the parent or guardian of the child needing treatment are responsible for weighing the risks before beginning any of the therapies described in this book. The author assumes no responsibility for inaccuracies, omissions or errors contained in the source materials. The author and publisher are not liable for the use or misuse of information provided.

2nd Edition—Revised and Updated

Printed in the United States of America

ISBN 978-1732407329
eBook ISBN 978-1732407336

Cover Design by Silke Stein
Photos on Pages 38 & 214 © Garon Tornell used with permission
Improv Skit on page 211-212 used with permission from Shawn Amador

Dedication

To Don Nash who gave me my first journal and said, "Here write your stuff in here." And so I did.

To my sons. You are truly the light of my life!

Contents

Introduction	1
10 Truths about Autism Spectrum Disorder	5

FIRST STEPS

1) Tell Your Child He Has Autism Spectrum Disorder	10
Example ASD Fact Sheet	15
2) Create a "Comfy Place" Option	18
3) Instead of Saying "No," Teach Your Child This Important Phrase: "The Rule Is"	22
4) It Is Okay to Allow Your Child to Say, "No," to Sensory Input	26
5) Routine, Routine, Routine	33
6) Communicate, Communicate, Communicate	38
Special Section — Stimming	43
7) Allow and Encourage Your Child's One Track Hobbies and Collections	45
8) Choices, Choices, Choices	49
9) Meltdowns Will Happen—Be Prepared	55
Special Section — Teaching Safety	63
Special Section — Girl's with ASD	66
Special Section — Guest Parent Post	67
Special Section — Sleep	70
School	72
Diet	78
Social Time	81
Exercise	83

NEXT STEPS

1) Learn All You Can About The Helpful Stuff	88
2) Begin Moving Your Child Out of Her Comfort Zone	96
Special Section — Play Time	100
3) Social Stories	106
Special Section — Teaching Safety 2	115

4) Introduce New Sensations: Sensory Integration … **118**
    Special Section — Attitude Check … **126**
5) Slowly Introduce Changes in Routines … **127**
6) Show Your Child What Conversation Looks Like … **131**
7) Encourage Your Child to Try Something New … **137**
8) Begin to Give Your Child More Complicated Choices … **142**
9) Give Your Child the Tools He Needs for Self-Management … **147**
    Special Section — Nonverbal Children … **153**
    Special Section — Single Parents … **155**
School … **156**
Diet … **158**
Social Time … **160**
Exercise … **164**
    Services That Cost Money … **167**

CHALLENGE STEPS

1) Teach Your Child How to Help Himself Overcome ASD … **180**
    Special Section — Biomedical Interventions … **185**
2) Teach Your Child to Face and Solve Problems … **189**
3) Teach Your Child That Sometimes Rules Change … **193**
4) Teach Your Child How to Be Comfortable in the World of Sensations … **197**
5) Teach Your Child to Create His Own Routine and to Adjust … **202**
6) Teach Your Child the Nuances of Communication … **206**
    Special Section — Improv Games … **211**
    Special Section — Healing Diets … **213**
7) Teach Your Child to Use His Interests to Create and Meet Goals … **214**
8) Teach Your Child How to Step Out on Her Own … **218**
9) Teach Your Child How to Deal with a Build Up of Stress and Frustration … **223**
School … **228**
Diet … **230**
Social Time … **233**
Exercise … **235**
    Special Section — Where Do We Go From Here … **237**
    Special Section — Where Did We Begin? (Cameron's Story) … **239**
Index … **241**
About the Author … **245**

"Before I speak, I have something important to say."

—Groucho Marx

Introduction

About Us

Imagine if you will…It is Christmas, and six-year-old Cameron is darting about the room hugging strangers, opening other people's presents, rolling around on the floor, and talking in a forceful outdoor voice while indoors. He is like a whirling dervish.

This was a common scene for us. Cameron's second-grade teacher tried to convince me he had ADHD. As his mother, I knew him well, and as a teacher, I had worked with many children with ADHD. I knew this wasn't ADHD. But if not, then what was it? That was the question that weighed heavily on me like an elephant sitting on my chest. I used to compare Cameron to the Tasmanian Devil—always moving, spinning, in constant motion.

When Cameron was eight years old, after more than four years of asking, *What is this?* the "Aha" moment finally came. I realized his behaviors were incredibly similar to those I had seen in a person in my life who had autism. The pedantic speech and the light and touch sensitivity were clues. Both were very smart people, but social rules seemed beyond their comprehension. Armed with these thoughts, I asked the elementary school Cameron attended to test him. Thankfully, Asperger Syndrome (now called Autism Spectrum Disorder) was becoming a better-understood disorder, and at eight years old he was diagnosed. I was relieved! Finally, I had something to face head-on. I could do this! I was no longer facing an unknown situation. Yay!

Not yay. Unfortunately, there weren't any parent guides at the time and I could find nothing helpful on the internet. The school was marginally helpful, but they didn't have a program set up for kids who were smart and could learn but had severe social difficulties.

Not wanting to let this lack of resources to hold my son back, I set out to help him using my experience and training as a teacher along with sheer basic instinct. At first, it was very difficult. I didn't feel like I knew what I was doing. Others tried to give advice, but they didn't know my child like I did, and often the advice was in the form of negative feedback. If you would just discipline him more, he would behave... Have you been told that one before?

With each step forward, things got a little bit easier. Did we work hard? Oh, yes! There were tears and screaming and quite a few tantrums (from both Cameron and me), but slowly it paid off. Now, you would have to spend quite a bit of time with Cameron before you would notice any of his Asperger's characteristics. Do I consider this success? Oh, yes! Would I have changed my child and taken away his Asperger's in the beginning if I could? No way! Why not? Because I have enjoyed every moment of his unique and complex personality. He has helped me to grow as a person, he has made me laugh (often), and he has brought tears of joy to my eyes. In so many ways, children with Autism Spectrum Disorder are no different than other children. They simply take longer to learn certain things and see the world through a different filter.

We didn't have a coach, any therapists outside of school, or specialists. We had no guides or rules to follow. So how did we do it? I tried one thing or another that simply made sense. I used what worked and discarded what didn't. And I took advantage of every resource I could get my hands on along the way, including a few patient and understanding teachers.

My son was a teenager when I wrote the first edition of this book. This month, he graduated from college with an art degree. On top of that, he worked full time all four years of school in order to help support his family. He regularly goes out with friends. Next, he will be starting an electrical engineering apprenticeship.

Success? Oh yes!

About This Book

As an educator, I had plenty of training throughout my career on how to work with children. I thought this would give me an advantage. Instead, the most important thing I learned on our journey with ASD is, no matter the hurdle, anything can be accomplished if taken one step at a time. In this guide, I offer you many of those steps.

Begin with today only. The good news is, you don't need to worry about tomorrow just yet. Put some First Steps into practice now so tomorrow will be easier. Work to find some peace and calm before tackling goals toward success.

When that is accomplished, move on to the Next Steps. Begin building up your child's world and then integrating him into the world. Finally, when you are ready, use the Challenge Steps to help your child gain independence. This is when things can get really exciting!

Don't worry if you feel one of the steps is taking too long. Each child moves at his or her own pace. Also, feel free to jump ahead in one area when you are ready, but stay in the First Steps for everything else. Not all aspects of your life will necessarily move at the same pace.

Throughout the book, I have also included dozens of the very best books, out of the hundreds I have read, for further reference and help.

Remember: Every child is different. Use what tips work for your family and cross off what doesn't. Or, if something doesn't work the first time, try it again in a few months and see what happens. It is possible you weren't ready the first time.

Be patient, work hard, laugh a lot, and take one day at a time.

Note: I found it was easier to use the same pronouns consistently throughout each section of the book, then change it for the next section. Please insert the pronoun that applies to you as you read. I also use the term ASD child. I found I prefer this general term over many of the alternatives such as neuro-atypical or aspie.

Also Note: I am not a medical or mental health professional. When in doubt or in need, please seek the advice of these professionals in your life.

Important Tip

Because every child is different and has varied needs, each section of steps in this book will require the right amount of time it takes for YOUR child to complete the tasks. This could take weeks or months. Do not feel you have to push your child to achieve each step. Move forward only when you feel your child is ready.

10 Truths About Autism Spectrum Disorder

1) The number one most important truth about ASD is that it is not your fault. As a matter of fact, blame is not necessary or helpful to your family as you work towards healing for your child. So please don't go there. There is most likely no way to know how your child got ASD. There are plenty of theories. However, the belief is beginning to shift towards the cause being a combination of factors which may include genetics, the environment, and the immune system. To complicate matters, ASD can be caused by different factors in different individuals.

2) Asperger's Syndrome and Pervasive Developmental Disorder (PDD) are no longer diagnosed in the U.S. They are now lumped together with Autism under the diagnosis of Autism Spectrum Disorder. There are positives and negatives to this change, but one truth of it stands out. Autism is a **spectrum** disorder. This means children can have different types of symptoms along the spectrum of varying degrees. No two children with autism are alike. Therefore, an individualized treatment approach is vital to success.

3) Children with Autism Spectrum Disorder tend to have many of the following characteristics:
    - Difficulty understanding social situations
    - Difficulty making and keeping friends
    - Difficulty understanding creative language and body language

- Difficulty with language skills
- Difficulty with motor skills
- A Narrow range of interests and insistence on routines
- Sensory sensitivities
- Difficulty with self-regulation
- Average to above average intelligence (not always easily measured)
- Use of repetitive behaviors (stimming)
- Appear disconnected from the world around them

4) ASD is a disorder, not a disease (illness). This means it is not something someone else can catch and at this time it is not something the doctors can look at under the microscope and declare it to be autism based on the results. Instead, doctors must look at characteristics and stages of development for a diagnosis.

5) Your child is wonderfully and beautifully made! Don't let anyone tell you otherwise. He or she is not broken, deficient, damaged, or incomplete. Children with ASD have minds that work in incredible and fascinating ways. Look for the ways your child sees the world as unique and delightful!

6) ASD is becoming more common. What was once a diagnosis of one child out of every ten thousand has become one out of sixty-eight children![1] This number has increased about twenty-five percent from five years ago.

7) ASD is treatable. There is no cure in the form of a medicine or one treatment that fits all for ASD; however, there are treatments for the various symptoms of ASD that can significantly reduce or eliminate them.

8) Although early intervention may grant you better future success for your child, it is **never** too late to begin. Your child can learn at any age.

9) Your child has emotions. He may not know how to process or to express them, but they exist. Your child can be taught how to process and express them.

10) Your child wants to connect. Although your child seems to live in a world all his own and enjoy it, he doesn't want to stay there. There are many factors that may be affecting his ability to connect. Show him the way to bridge the gap, keeping him from connecting, and he will happily meet you there.

---

1. Five years ago, the number was reported by the CDC (Centers for Disease Control and Prevention) as one in eighty-eight children based on the following Report:

Baio, J. Prevalence of Autism Spectrum Disorders--Autism and Developmental Disabilities Monitoring Network, 14 Sites, United States, 2008. Surveillance Summaries, March 30, 2012.

"Don't walk in front of me;
I may not follow.
Don't walk behind me;
I may not lead.
Just walk beside me
and be my friend."

—Albert Camus

FIRST STEPS

In the beginning, you will need to create calm. Take a step back, take a breath, and then begin to figure things out. At this point, take the pressure off yourself. Don't feel like you have to do or fix anything. Instead, begin by creating a calm environment for your child. Learn about your child. Spend time observing and getting to know him. This will give you a more clear perspective from which to help him as you progress through the steps to success.

1

Tell Your Child He Has Autism Spectrum Disorder

Why?

The truth is, your child most likely already knows he is a little bit different. People may not treat him the same as others or may say something to point it out. He may feel bad about being different and needs to hear from you that there is nothing wrong with him, that he is unique and has a lot of special qualities. Now, and in the future, he will hear you talking about ASD. Telling him about it will give him a context to work with.

At Home

- ☐ Look at the book list on page 16. Encourage your child to read for himself about ASD. Better yet, read one of these books with him and discuss what ASD means.

- ☐ Stress over and over to your child that he is not wrong, a weirdo, abnormal, stupid, a freak, retarded, or any other horrible names that have been used. Stress that your child's brain has a unique way of looking at the world. It may different from others, but many smart and famous people like Albert Einstein and Dr. Temple Grandin had unique ways of seeing the world. And look at what they have accomplished!

- ☐ Talk to your child about some of the ways you are going to help him make sense of the world and become more comfortable from sensitivities.

- ☐ Don't worry if your child denies or ignores that he has ASD. It may take a while for it to sink in or for him to be okay with the diagnosis. Give him time.

- ☐ Regardless of how your child feels about things, validate his feelings. Don't try to make him feel any particular way about having ASD.

- ☐ Talk to your child about his positive qualities and strengths.

- ☐ Stress how much you love your child and want to help him. Make sure he knows that you don't want to change him or turn him into someone else. You simply want to make things easier and better for him.

Family

- ☐ Tell your child's siblings, aunts, uncles, grandparents, etc. about ASD. Keep the explanation very simple. Explain that there will be some things that need to be done differently to make your child comfortable and this, in turn, will make everyone else more comfortable.

- ☐ Emphasize to your family that your child cannot help his behaviors. He is doing the best he can. the cause of ASD is not as important as understanding what it means to have it.

- ☐ Be aware that some family members will not *buy in* to this diagnosis. At this point agree to disagree. Eventually, they will see what ASD means as you work to help your child.

- ☐ If someone says to you, "You just need to discipline him more and he will behave!" Simply ask, "How will that work?" Many people are quick to give simple solutions to things which they don't understand.

- ☐ Keep the blame for the cause of your child's ASD out of the conversation, as this will not help. There is no blame to be placed.

Siblings

- ☐ **Do** tell your other children about ASD if they are old enough to understand. There are great picture books available to help with this for younger children. (see page 16) Keep the explanation simple and talk about what it will mean to help your child with ASD.

- ☐ Don't make your other children carry responsibility for your ASD child above what is normally expected. This can cause them a lot of stress as well as guilt if they can't always succeed in helping.

☐ Take special time out to be alone with your other children. Your ASD child will require more attention, especially in the beginning. This can be hard on his siblings. Create dates where you can spend time together. If there is more than one sibling, have a separate date with each child so he or she enjoys that special individualized attention.

Who Else?

Tell anyone in close regular contact with your child about his ASD. This might be a Sunday School teacher, sports coach, teacher (we'll talk more about school later), parents in a regular playgroup, daycare teachers, doctors, tutors, and so on. Talk to these people about any considerations that may need to be made on behalf of your child. But keep explanations simple, giving only the most helpful and necessary information. It may take a lot of your time to talk to each person, but extra time now will mean more comfort later.

Important Tip

Consider typing a short fact sheet about ASD to pass out to those in your child's life. This was especially helpful when Cameron was older and had several teachers. I could give them the sheet, tell them he was on an IEP (Individual Education Plan), and ask them to contact me if there were any problems. Before I began using the sheet, I would get calls from teachers concerned about problem behaviors. When I explained about the Asperger's, their tone would change to understanding. I quickly learned that the fact sheet headed off a lot of problems that might have come up if the teachers hadn't known the facts about my child ahead of time. (see page 15)

Become An Expert On Your Child

In the Next Steps section, you will be creating a plan to help your child on this journey. Begin now by getting to know your child better. What are his strengths, difficulties, and needs? How does he learn best? What does he avoid? What does he enjoy? What does he dislike? What is his learning style? Begin a journal and write down the answers to these questions as you observe them. You will use this information later.

Cameron's Corner

"It took a while to fully understand what it meant to have Asperger's. Knowing that Asperger's is about having a difficult time with social skills helped me to take steps to put myself out there socially."

Example Fact Sheet

My child, Cameron O'Hair, has Asperger's also called Autism Spectrum Disorder. This means he has trouble with social skills and may show behaviors and interests that are sometimes different from other children. Cameron is very smart and a hard worker, but may take longer to learn some of the more common sense things.

These are some things Cameron has the most trouble with right now:

*Sitting still in class (drumming on the desks and tables)
*Changes in routines, rules, or schedules
*Asking for help
*Difficulty with loud noises and lots of people
*Learning new rules and routines in class
*Being publicly corrected

Please feel free to talk to me about any behaviors or difficulties that may be a concern to you. I will be happy to help him with this at home. Here are some things that will help my son to be more comfortable and better able to learn:

*Agree on a signal between him and you if his drumming becomes bothersome
*Let him know ahead of time before any major changes occur
*Let him decide whether to attend assemblies
*Preferred seating
*Asking him at the end of class if he has any questions
*Correct his behavior privately

Thank you for understanding and helping my amazing son to thrive!

Book Nook

All Cats Have Asperger Syndrome (picture book)
by Kathy Hoopmann
(A cute and encouraging book using pictures of cats to explain Aspergers)

Inside Aspergers Looking Out (picture book)
by Kathy Hoopmann
(An adorable book written to explain Aspergers)

This is Asperger Syndrome (picture book)
by Brenda Smith Myles & Elisa Gagnon
("Experience the world from the perspective of a young child with AS")

Ten Things Every Child with Autism Wishes You Knew (2nd ed.)
by Ellen Notbohm
(A short guide explaining the basics of ASD. Would be great to give to teachers, family members etc.)

My Brother Charlie (picture book)
by Holly Robinson Peete, Ryan E. Peete, & Shane Evans
(A sister's story about her autistic brother)

Asperger's Huh? A Child's Perspective (picture book)
by Rosina Schnurr & John Strachan
(A good simple book explaining aspergers to an older child) No longer in print, but copies are available on Amazon

Autism and Me—Sibling Stories (picture book)
by Ouisie Shapiro

My Friend Has Autism (picture book)
by Amanda Doering Tourville
(Explains autism to children or siblings)

I Know Someone With Autism (picture book)
by Sue Barraclough
("This book introduces readers to what autism is, how it affects people, and what they can do to be a good friend to someone living with autism")

Understanding Brothers and Sisters on the Autism Spectrum
DVD by Coulter Video
(Has different sections for different age audiences)

2

Create A "Comfy Place" Option

Why?

Your child is in a constant state of being overwhelmed and confused. To her, things look different, feel different, and sound different. She doesn't always understand what you are trying to communicate. This can make her anxious and scared. Imagine being in a room full of roaring lions, hissing snakes, and charging bulls. What would you do? Run? Hide? Would you really stop and think your way out of the situation? Sometimes, your child needs a quiet place to escape the overwhelming world for a time.

At Home

- ☐ Explore ideas of where your child could go where she feels safe and calm? Her bedroom perhaps? Maybe the closet floor would be even better since it is quiet and dark. Not enough room? How about a decorated cardboard box, a small child's tent or a bed tent? Or she could pile a bunch of pillows on the floor. You could also try a sleeping bag or bean bag chair that travels with her when you go away overnight.

- ☐ Talk to your child and explain that everyone likes a quiet place to be by themselves sometimes. Tell her your favorite place. Ask where in the house she would feel most comfortable and let her claim it for herself.

- ☐ Allow your child to decorate her space and give it a special name. Let her put her favorite comfy items there such as pillows, stuffed animals, music, a night light, etc.

- ☐ Does your child feel calm when rocking? Get her a child-sized rocking chair or an adult sized one if she is bigger.

- ☐ Never use your child's comfy place as a place of punishment or time-out. This place is meant for happiness and comfort where your child can learn self-soothing techniques. If you use time-out, make it happen somewhere other than the comfy place. This way, when your child goes to the comfy place, she can relax and when she goes to time-out she knows she needs to think about and correct her behavior.

☐ If your child has some regular comfort items, create a special spot in her room where she can put these away herself so she will always know where they are.

Out and About

☐ Talk to your child ahead of time about a comfy place she can use when out and about. Might the car be an option? If she is a smaller child, how about in the shopping cart with a jacket or favorite blanky over her head? Be creative!

☐ Put together a "Comfy" Travel Bag to take with you wherever you go. This should contain her favorite snacks, water, handheld games, comfy blanket or stuffed animal, as well as any items needed to cut down on sensory noise (see chapter #4, beginning on page 26 for more on sensory issues).

Important Tip

Agree with your child on a reasonable time limit for being in her comfy spot before she has to rejoin the world. It is important to spend time relaxing, but it is easy for the comfy spot to become a crutch.

Visiting Homes

Call the person ahead of time and explain that sometimes your child feels overwhelmed and may need a quiet place to chill for a little bit. Ask if they have somewhere safe in their home like this. Then explain to your child, before going, what is available to her if at any time she needs a comfy spot to relax.

At School

- ☐ Ask your child's teacher to provide a comfy spot. This is extremely important, since kids with ASD often get overwhelmed at school. Old fashioned desk carrels are excellent—your child can still work but be closed off from some of the extra input. Even under a table can be a great relief for a little while.

- ☐ Talk to the teacher about allowing her to bring one comfort item to school to be used during times of stress.

Cameron's Corner

"Our home is so small I really have nowhere to go so I wear headphones with my favorite music to tune out the world. I bring my iPod and headphones everywhere too. If your space is small, think of different ways to create a comfy place. Also, I keep a separate backpack filled with all my most important items. I take this almost everywhere."

3

Instead Of Saying, "No," Teach Your Child This Important Phrase: The Rule Is

Why?

Children with ASD are concrete logical thinkers. They become confused and frustrated when they don't understand the rules of a situation. Once they *get* the rules, they know how to *play* the game.

At Home

- ☐ In every situation possible, teach him the rules of your home. "The rule at our table is, we eat out food, not play with it.", "The rule is, we pick up and put away our toys before doing something else.", "The rule is, we take a bath every day. We brush our teeth morning and night. We get dressed before leaving the house," etc. Be very specific and detailed about each rule.

- ☐ Begin with simple rules that are most important for keeping your child and home safe and comfortable.

- ☐ Don't say "don't." If you say, "Don't take a toy from your friend without asking," your child will think, "Why not? I want the toy, I can have it!" He needs to learn there are rules that run the world, and to get along well, he will have to follow them. "**The rule is**, we ask for toys we want to play with."

- ☐ If your child makes a mistake, feel free to ask, "Elliot, what is the rule about sitting on the couch?" Hopefully, he will remember and correct his mistake. If not, repeat the rule, "The rule is, couches are for sitting on or laying on only."

- ☐ Have rules that never change in your house such as rules regarding safety, rules about hygiene (daily baths, brushing teeth, etc.), and rules about fighting.

Out and About

Throughout everything you do, create opportunities to teach the rules of everyday living.

- "The rule is, we use a quiet talking voice in stores."
- "The rule is, we can't take things out of the store unless we pay for them."
- "The rule is we must always stay in the car seat or have our seat belt on while the car is moving."

Visiting Homes

Ask your friends and family to use the phrase, "The rule is," to help teach your child the important rules of the world.

- "The rule is, we knock on the door and wait to be invited in before entering."
- "The rule is, we walk when we are inside."

Social Situations

Although your child may not be socializing much yet, begin teaching the rules now at every opportunity so that when he does begin to join groups, he will have the basics stored in his memory.

- "The rule is, we take turns talking."
- "The rule is, we often share with others."
- "The rule is, we ask to play with someone else's toy."
- "The rule is, we use words when angry, instead of biting or hitting."

Important Tip

Your child will need to hear these rules over and over before they all sink in. There is quite a list to learn and remember! Continue to patiently repeat the rules that your child has not mastered and eventually he will put them into practice.

Expect Mistakes! Celebrate effort!

At School

Ask your child's teacher to use the phrase, "The rule is," to keep things consistent. Help your child to understand that rules change according to where you are. The rules he is used to at home may not be the rules he follows at school.

Final Note

In the Next Steps section, starting on page 106, you will learn about Social Stories which will further help you to teach rules.

Cameron's Corner

"Now, I ask my peers and elders for what to do and not to do in a new situation. If a kid is too embarrassed to ask, he can learn a lot from posted information like class rules or a class syllabus or he can ask his parents to give him the information."

4

It Is Okay To Allow Your Child To Say, "No," To Sensory Input

Why?

Remember, the ASD child is overwhelmed by the world. She may be oversensitive to certain sensations. Sensory issues are different for every child. Helping your child to eliminate the most difficult sensations will give her much appreciated relief. This will allow her to feel more relaxed, as well as ready and able to connect and learn.

At Home

- ☐ Understand that your child may not like to be touched. This includes hugs, kisses, tickling, etc. And although she may give hugs to random strangers, giving and receiving touch are two very different things. Learn what touches your child does and does not like.

- ☐ Tell your child, that for you, hugging and kissing your child is one way you like to show you love her. Find out what touch she could accept that you could use to show your love, such as touching your hand to her head or a high five.

- ☐ Buy bedding and furnishings for her room in colors and textures most comfortable to her.

- ☐ Try 100% cotton bedding or another all natural fiber.

- ☐ Allow your child to pick out her clothing for herself. If a younger child, let her feel each article of clothing before you buy it. You can usually tell by her reaction if the clothing will be comfortable.

- ☐ If your child is touch sensitive, cut tags out of all clothing. She will probably tear them out herself and leave holes if you don't neatly cut them first.

- ☐ If your child is given a clothing item as a gift and throws a fit, refusing to wear it, understand that the color or feel of it may be too harsh for her. Teach her how to deal with this situation in a kind manner toward the giver.

- [ ] Allow your child to decide how to decorate her room even if it seems odd to you. Every child has a different sense of what is comfortable.

- [ ] Consider a smaller wattage light bulb in her bedroom lamp if she is sensitive to light. Don't buy fluorescent light bulbs. These are especially hard on the eyes.

- [ ] Consider a dimmer switch in her bedroom. Then your child can adjust the light as she needs.

- [ ] If a lot of sunlight comes in through her bedroom window, consider heavier curtains or blackout blinds.

- [ ] Use soap, shampoo, lotion, laundry detergent, etc. for sensitive skin and in scents your child likes.

- [ ] Be careful of chemicals used in your home as these can strongly affect a sensitive child. Look for more natural options when possible such as natural cleaning supplies.

- [ ] Allow your child to wear ear muffs or headphones when sound becomes overwhelming, especially in public.

- [ ] Allow your child to be picky about foods as long as she is willing to try one bite of new foods occasionally.

- [ ] Check the brightness on televisions and computers. Make sure they are not set to an overly bright setting. Consider a glare filter for the computer if your child spends a lot of time at the computer, or possibly computer glasses only to be worn when working at the computer. (ask her eye doctor about this.)

- [ ] Provide a way to listen to calming sounds such as an iPod with favorite music or nature sounds, or use a noise machine.

- [ ] Find out what stimuli is soothing to your child by watching what activities she engages in to calm herself. Encourage these things.

- ☐ If your child likes pressure for calming, buy several floor pillows that she can pile on top of herself when she wants to have some calming time.

- ☐ Or consider weighted items such as blankets, vests, lap pads, or stuffed animals. Search the internet to find merchants who sell weighted items. **For safety, make sure these items are the correct weight for your child. Let an expert help you determine this.** Once you know the correct weight, these are items that could be made at home.

- ☐ **Never force your child to make eye contact with anyone**. Making eye contact is often very difficult and painful for ASD children to do. Pressing the issue will merely add to your child's distress. In most cases, she will be better able to listen if she is not forced to concentrate her eyes on you at the same time. The ability to make eye contact will come later.

- ☐ Allow your child to continue to use stimming techniques such as noises, rocking and hand flapping, for now. As you cut down on difficult sensations, observe if the stimming decreases.

- ☐ Turn off the television and other electronic devices when they are not in use to cut down on background noise. Even the humming of a plugged-in radio can bother over-sensitive children.

- ☐ Consider removing all devices that run on electricity from your child's bedroom. If you keep an electric clock in her bedroom, put it on the side of the room farthest from her bed.

- ☐ Begin each day in a soothing manner with no television. Mornings are often hectic and rushed, and noise from the television on top of that can make them even more difficult.

- ☐ Create a quiet time an hour before bed when all televisions and electronic devices are turned off and everyone is engaged in more quiet activities such as reading, quiet music, and a bedtime routine.

Out and About

☐ Teach your child that it is okay to tell people that she doesn't like to be hugged or touched. This also helps teach self-safety which is very important.

☐ Allow your child to wear sunglasses—even indoors—to cut down on bright lights. This is especially needed for sunny days and in buildings with an abundance of fluorescent lights.

☐ Let your child wear headphones with portable music. Providing her favorite music would be especially helpful for bringing some comfort wherever she goes.

☐ Allow your child to chew gum, if it feels calming when she is overwhelmed.

☐ Bring her favorite snacks with you—just in case. Kids always seem to be hungry!

Visiting Homes

☐ Explain that other family members like to give hugs and kisses, too. Talk to your child about a way to deal with this ahead of time such as putting her hand out for a handshake if she would prefer that to a hug.

☐ Teach this rule: "The rule is, when you are offered a food you don't like or want, simply say, 'no thank you,' or take it anyway, but don't eat it."

☐ Explain to friends and family why your child might sometimes wear headphones or sunglasses or complain about particular sensations. Help them to understand how these things can be painful to your child and are not just a preference.

At School

- ☐ Ask the teacher to provide preferred seating for your child which means the spot in the room where your child is most comfortable.

- ☐ Ask the school to give your child the option to skip assemblies and events with crowds.

- ☐ Talk to your child's teacher about her sensory needs.

- ☐ Work with your child to provide the best sack lunch possible. If she is old enough, expect her to make her own lunch (with some rules of course).

- ☐ If your child eats a school lunch, talk to the school cafeteria about her special nutrition needs. Some school cafeterias require students to have certain things on the tray or other rules. Request that they exempt your child from these rules. The cafeteria is required to make accommodations. They may require something in writing, but it is worth taking the time.

Important Tip

Be encouraged. Sensory issues will improve over time. The goal right now is to make your child as comfortable as possible. However, be sure your child takes regular breaks from headphones, ear plugs, or sunglasses, as prolonged use can affect regular sensory development.

Book Nook

The Out of Sync Child
by Carol Stock Kranowitz
(Discusses sensory processing disorders)

Cameron's Corner

"I can't handle tight or itchy clothes so I like to shop for myself. If something doesn't feel good I won't wear it. I don't like certain types of music so I avoid it or use my own headphones to cover it up. Bright lights are also a problem for me. I am learning to wear sunglasses more when I need them. The hardest thing for me sometimes is small noises at night that keep me awake. I like to put pillows close to my ears to muffle sounds."

5

Routine, Routine, Routine

Why?

Children with ASD thrive with structure and routine because a structured world is one they have already processed and are familiar with. Anything new in their lives requires new and possibly difficult processing work. Following a schedule and telling them what to expect eases the fear and frustration that might come with change. ASD children can also become very focused on an activity. Changing from that activity to another can be as difficult for them as going from a hot tub to an ice-cold swimming pool.

At Home

- ☐ If your child is not yet reading, use your digital camera to take pictures of familiar items and create a visual schedule or a taskbar showing what activities are to be done and in what order.

- ☐ Keep a family activity calendar. If your child can read, place as many scheduled events on the calendar as possible.

- ☐ Create a morning routine and a bedtime routine for the whole family to follow. This will not only help your child with ASD, but will create more peace during these often hectic times.

- ☐ Always give your child a 5 or 10-minute warning before he will have to switch gears to a new activity. Setting a timer is an excellent concrete way to give him the warning.

- ☐ Establish a departure routine when you leave your child somewhere or when you leave the house. Never sneak away, as this leads to distrust. Discuss ahead of time with your child the times when you will need to go away. Tell him how long you will be gone. Tell him what it might mean if you are late and what to do if that happens. Assure him you are coming back. If he doesn't like hugs, establish a contact he does like and tell him you do that because you will miss him while you are gone.

- If moving furniture, cleaning a room, doing home maintenance, or otherwise upsetting the physical balance of the home, tell your child what's going to happen and why. Reassure him that his comfy spot will still be available.

- If your child cannot handle someone else touching his things, and you do the cleaning, consider cleaning his room while he's away. Or, if he prefers, only clean his room when he can watch and supervise. Give him some of the power of telling you exactly how things can be moved and cleaned. As soon as he is old enough, it is best to teach him how to do all the cleaning by himself so he won't have to worry about who is touching or moving his things.

- If someone comes over for a visit, tell your child that in five minutes you would like him to stop what he is doing in order to say hello.

Out and About

- Before leaving the house for errands or activities, give your child a play by play schedule of where you will be going and what you will be doing. It helps if you can throw a few possible difficulties in that you might encounter. Something like this: "We will get in the car and drive to the grocery store to buy groceries. Sometimes we have to wait in line. Then we will drive to the library where we will return our books and movies and pick out some new ones. Remember, the limit is only two books. Then we will drive to see my friend Maria where you can play with her daughter Suzie for a little while. Then we will drive home." Although most ASD kids have exceptional memories, sometimes they can get sidetracked. To help, at the end of each errand, remind your child where you are going next. If he can read, consider writing everything out as a list and allowing your child to check each item off after it has been completed.

- Don't alter the schedule unless absolutely necessary. This throws the ASD child from the world he has already processed into the chaos of having to figure out the change. If you must make an unexpected stop, make sure your child knows ahead of time what the change will be. Trust me, if you start driving to the gas station instead of the library he will know!

☐ When going to a new place you've never gone to before, tell your child where you are going and what you are going to do there. Try to explain a little about the place if you can. Reassure him that his comfy place or travel bag is available wherever you go.

☐ If you have promised your child you would take him somewhere, but you have to change plans, explain ahead of the scheduled time why you have had to make the change. Tell him how important you know the trip is and if possible offer to reschedule. Place it on the family calendar right then to reinforce its importance. If, after your best efforts, a tantrum follows, ride it out. It is impossible to hold back all disruptions in routine, and your child will have to work through some of this.

Visiting Homes

☐ Give a 5 or 10-minute warning before it is time to leave.

☐ Ask friends and family to also give this 5 or 10-minute warning when it is time to change from one activity to another.

Important Tip

Everybody likes routine—your favorite morning cup of coffee, the daily exercise, regular calls to your spouse. These make you happy. Find which activities make your child happy and encourage him to build these into his routine. Keep these as consistent as possible especially as other routine items may have to change at some point.

School

- ☐ Create a written schedule your child can follow. Ask his teacher to let him know ahead of time if there will be a change of schedule.

- ☐ Make a picture schedule if your child is not yet reading.

- ☐ If the teacher knows ahead of time, ask her to tell your child when a substitute will be in charge. Make sure your child knows what that means and how to respond to it. Tell him the schedule will be different on substitute days. If he is prepared for this change ahead of time it will be like a scheduled change.

- ☐ Talk to your child's school about emergency drills and how your child can be accommodated. This may mean letting your child know ahead of time or allowing him to be with a different teacher or in a more comfortable place.

Cameron's Corner

"In my life, I like to plan out everything ahead of time. Things need to be scheduled out hours, to a full day in advance, sometimes perfectly to the minute. When plans change or something takes longer than expected I get really frustrated and have to calm down before proceeding."

6

Communicate, Communicate, Communicate

This young man's dad told him, "Just stack them somewhere."
Dad got exactly what he asked for.

Why?

Good communication does not come naturally to the child with ASD. Some do better with non-verbal communication; others do not. Either way, they need to be shown how to express themselves to get what they want. It is also important to communicate with them in a specific way to get what you want from them.

How?

- ☐ Speak slowly and precisely to your child. Do not add extra unnecessary words to your instructions as this can add confusion. Say exactly what you mean. For instance, instead of saying, "Throw your stuff in the laundry room," say, "Put your dirty clothes in the hamper in the laundry room." The ASD child will think literally about the first statement and you may get exactly that—clothes thrown into the room.

- ☐ Use clear language free of idioms like *"quiet as a mouse"* or *"I'm all thumbs."*

- ☐ Never talk baby talk to your child. This will slow down the learning process and will not model proper conversation.

- ☐ **Neither expect nor force eye contact.** Simply because your child is not looking at you does not mean she is not listening or processing what you are saying. Many children with ASD literally *cannot* give you eye contact. In many cases, it is incredibly painful. Instead, give her plenty of time to process what you are saying and ask for some cue that she understood you—such as a nod of the head. Even if she nods her head, be prepared that you may later need to repeat what you said.

- ☐ Be careful about using absolute language. Words such as: **always**, **never**,

forever, all, none, every, only, and **must** suggest that there are no exceptions.

- [ ] Get creative and speak your child's language. If she often uses phrases from movies, television shows, and books, then use them too when conversing. This is a great way to connect.

- [ ] Remember, when communicating, the child with ASD has several things going on in her brain that may hinder understanding. First, she may be concentrating on other things even though she may appear to be listening. Second, she is a logical thinker. If you use creative language (such as idioms and slang), she may get lost. Third, your child has difficulty switching gears quickly. If her mind is on something else, it may take her a little bit of work to switch to listening to what you are saying.

- [ ] Begin with one-step instructions. Instead of saying, "Please put away your toys, put on your pajamas, and brush your teeth for bed," try, "It is time for bed. Put away your toys. Then I will tell you what is next. But first, put away the toys" (a repeat).

- [ ] Give specific instructions instead of general ones. Instead of saying, "Put away your toys," break up the steps by saying, "It's clean-up time. First, put your blocks in the blocks tub. Next, put your books on the bookshelf." Or even better would be to practice choice making. "Which would you choose to put away first—your blocks or your books?" "Which would you choose to put away next—your blocks or your cars?"

Out and About

Be an interpreter for your child when in public. Help her understand what people are saying to her by breaking it down. Help her communicate with others if you understand what she is saying, but others do not. You can be a temporary link between your child and others until she learns how to make the connections herself.

Visiting Homes

Help others understand your child's communication needs. Model ways they can better communicate with your child and ways to teach her how to communicate. Don't be shy! Turn everyone around you into a teacher for your child.

Important Tip

Constantly narrate what you and your child are doing. If you are cooking in the kitchen while your ASD child is there, mirror with words what you are doing. "First, I will get out the mixing bowl. Now I need the egg beaters. I'm getting the eggs and milk out of the fridge. You are holding the mixer and mixing the eggs." This helps your child to make a stronger connection between her and you and the activities you are both engaged in.

School

Talk to your child's teacher about her communication needs. Find out if speech therapy would be appropriate. Speech therapists work with children on the meaning of words, when to use certain words, memorization, creative language and more.

Cameron's Corner

"When talking to your child, first make sure you are getting his attention since his mind may be elsewhere. Don't use idioms like "it drives me up the wall," since kids like us don't understand these until someone teaches them to us. Be very specific with your words and repeat what you say to make sure he got it. Sometimes, I need people to repeat things to me so I can fully understand."

Special Section—Stimming

Stimming is short for self-stimulatory behavior. This can include behaviors such as rocking, jumping, hand flapping, spinning, making the same noise over and over, putting the same things in order over and over, tics, blinking in a different manner, staring, rubbing, scratching, OCD (obsessive compulsive) tendencies. or, in my son's case, drumming on anything and everything and whistling.

There are two theories for the reason why kids with ASD stim. One is that the stimming is a way to stimulate the senses if they are hypo-sensitive (under-sensitive). Another is that the stimming is a way to drown out everything else around them if they are hyper-sensitive (over-sensitive). It is possible for a child to be hypo-sensitive with some of his senses and hyper-sensitive with others.

For many parents, stimming drives them crazy and often embarrasses them in public. Some parents worry that stimming isn't normal and wonder whether it should be allowed.

There are stimming behaviors which are beneficial and there are others which are harmful. Lessening the harmful ones is the goal. For instance, I enjoy having my hair brushed, but if I brush my hair all day long, I will soon go bald. A good action can thus be turned into something harmful. A child who rocks back and forth to soothe himself may not be receiving the benefit of the action when it is nonstop. Instead, this may increase the agitation.

Other stims are simply expressions of emotions such as hand flapping when happy or grunting when angry. These stims are normally short in duration.

Step back and observe what kinds of stimming your child is engaging in. What senses is he stimulating? Is he rubbing on things (touch)? Is he blinking all the time (visual)? Next, pay attention to when he is most often engaging in these behaviors. Is it mostly when he is in public or around other people? Does he do it when loud noises happen? Are the actions comforting or do they seem to agitate him further?

The following suggestions apply to stims used to calm or stimulate, not to stims which are expressions of emotions. Expressions of emotions are a treasure and using stims is a great place for your child to start showing others how he feels

First

For now, let your child stim. It is one of the best tools in his toolbox, and he doesn't yet have all the tools he needs to filter the sensations around him. Taking away the stims without replacing them with something healthier may be devastating. By trying to force your child to stop stimming, you may cause him additional stress which may then make him stim more. In the Next Steps section, we will talk about sensory integration which should help your child stim less and less. (see page 118)

Next

As your child begins to become calmer, talk to him about his stims and how they might bother people when he does them in public. Talk to him about trying to stim only at home and come up with ways to deal with sensory overload when he is in public. Talk about how the stims make him feel. Do they comfort him or do they make him feel worse? Agree on better ways for him to calm himself if the stims are not helpful. Allow him to stim freely if his stress level gets unmanageable.

Challenge

Use sensory integration techniques as suggested in the Next Steps section. Work to discover which activities calm your child. Encourage your child to engage in calming activities at home. Again, discuss stimming in public with your child. Don't put him down or make him feel bad as these are mostly behaviors he can't help. Work together on ways to replace the behavior(s) with something else more appropriate for use in public such as chewing gum, using a smoothing stone in his jacket pocket, tapping quietly on his leg, quiet foot tapping, or walking around.

7

Allow And Encourage Your Child's One Track Hobbies And Collections

Why?

An ASD child's brain locks on to certain subjects in what may seem an obsessive way. Encouraging these subjects in different areas of his life helps him to make connections between that which is familiar and comfortable, and new information. It can also be a great way to make social connections.

At Home

- ☐ Create a special place for your child to keep information on his favorite subject(s) or a place to play with his favorite items. If the topic of the month is trains, then make a train station where everything is stored.

- ☐ Work together to organize everything he collects on his topic. Create notebooks for written information, use labeled tubs for storage, etc. This is a perfect opportunity to teach organizational skills.

- ☐ If reading is a difficult skill for your child, find books on his favorite topic at an appropriate reading level with which to practice.

- ☐ Decorate his world with his favorite subject. If he loves dinosaurs, find a dinosaur backpack, bedding, stickers, etc. This way he is surrounded by something he loves and makes him feel comfortable.

- ☐ In the Next Steps section, you will learn about Social Stories. Use your child's favorite subjects to create new Social Stories. (see page 106)

- ☐ Take every opportunity to use your child's favorite subjects to teach and to connect.

Out and About

Find places to take your child where he can learn more about his favorite subject, such as the library, museums, and special shows. This will be a wonderful way to practice being out in the world while he focuses primarily on something he loves. This narrow focus will help him shut out some of the world that causes distress.

At Other Homes

Allow your child to bring an item from his collections for comfort. Discuss ahead of time a limit on how much he can talk about his favorite subjects. Perhaps you can agree on an exact number of facts he can share with each person he talks to.

School

Ask your child's teacher to allow your child time with his favorite subjects as a reward for doing well in class. Encourage opportunities to share knowledge about his hobby with his classmates.

Important Tip

Your child's obsessions will most likely change over time, but then again, one may also become his profession!

Cameron's Corner

"When I was younger, I liked to collect things—a lot! Eventually, I became disinterested in that collection and moved on to something else. Now, I like to collect different kinds of music."

8

Choices, Choices, Choices

What?

There are a few books that I would recommend buying and reading over and over and this is one of them: ***Parenting with Love and Logic: Teaching Children Responsibility*** by Foster Cline, MD and Jim Fay. Also, check out their website at www.loveandlogic.com.

Why?

This book was life changing in how I was able to parent my ASD child. Our ASD children are logical thinkers.(And boy is this an amazing part of their personalities!) Love and Logic's® methods allow us to meet our children halfway and with respect. It teaches them how to teach themselves and learn how to solve their own problems. And of course, these strategies work well with all children of all ages and all types of thinking.

There are other behavior techniques that are offered to parents with children on the spectrum such as Applied Behavioral Analysis (ABA). These type of techniques that offer treats, prizes and praise for every "correct" behavior send some very confusing messages.

First, they tell the child that everything she believes to be correct must simply be wrong because she is being told she is wrong. This hurts her sense of self and increased confusion. One thing ASD children have in common is feeling the way they think is always right. Second, these methods teach that the child gets praised only when she pleases the adult. They never teach the child how to please herself or how to teach herself correct behavior. Take away the instruction and the praise and then what is the child supposed to do? She has little to no idea.

Teaching your child skills and behavior through love and with logic is a better way.

At Home

- [ ] First, Love and Logic® methods teach you to ask your child to be responsible for and empowered to make her own choices. This can be an especially difficult skill for an ASD child who is overwhelmed by her world. Begin by narrowing down the choices within acceptable boundaries. Acceptable to whom? Acceptable to you, the rule maker. For instance, if you want your child to pick up her toys, you might demand, "Pick up your toys!" In the ASD child's mind, she is thinking, "Why should I do that? It isn't what I want and isn't helpful to me." So instead, put some power in her court while still getting what you desire by asking, "Would you like to pick up your toys before your bath or after your bath?" Aha! She now gets to choose something that **does** matter to her. And you have given choices she can pick from that give you the desired outcome no matter which she chooses. She wins. You win.

- [ ] What if she says, "I don't want to pick up my toys!" You merely become a broken record and repeat, "The choices are…" Use the word "**choice**" as often as possible. This guides her to take responsibility by making a decision.

- [ ] Get your child's full attention before offering the choices.

- [ ] At mealtime, instead of asking, "What would you like to eat for lunch?" ask instead, "Would you like peanut butter and jelly or a tuna sandwich for lunch?" Again, this narrows down choices to a simple process—I choose either A or B—rather than thinking A through Z. And truly, open-ended questions can cause her to be thinking of A-Z with no answer coming any time soon.

- [ ] Create as many opportunities for your child as possible to practice making choices. Give her the choices, then step back and let her choose. Such as: "Would you like to carry your jacket or wear it to the park?" "Would you like a red or a blue toothbrush?" "Do you want a nap before your friend comes over or after?" The possibilities are endless!

☐ Begin teaching responsibility by expecting your child to complete some small regular chores. In the beginning, break them down into smaller parts.

☐ Have the same expectations for your child with ASD as you would any other child, but give her more time to accomplish them.

☐ In the book *Parenting with Love and Logic,* you will learn more about helping your child become responsible for her own behavior. This will be discussed more in the Next Steps section starting on page 142. For now, practice offering choices and see what this does to help calm your child and your home.

Out and About

Practice giving choices everywhere you go. "Would you like to help push the cart or to sit in the cart?" "Would you choose to go to the park with the swings or the park by the river?" The more you practice the more in control you will be.

At Other Homes

Model giving choices while in the homes of friends. For close friends and family members, discuss Love and Logic® practices and ask if they will help implement them with your child.

At School

Once you've begun putting Love and Logic® methods into practice, talk to your child's teacher about it. See if he would be willing to try it in the classroom. Tell him about the book, ***Teaching with Love and Logic: Taking Control of the Classroom*** for educators by Foster Cline and Jim Fay.

What Else?

Choose to remain positive at all times. Model this to your child. She will see and feel the difference. If you believe everything is going to work out well, she will believe the same. **Expect Success** in order to get it!

Important Tip

Practice, practice, practice. Work hard at not giving open-ended choices or choices that are actually threats. Before reading *Love and Logic***, out of frustration, I asked three-year-old Cameron, "Do you want a spanking?" He shocked me by replying, "Yes!" as he bent over to help me complete the task. I have no idea what his thought process was, but at that moment I knew I needed help with parenting this incredibly smart child!**

Book Nook

More great books from the *Love and Logic* family:

Parenting Children with Health Issues
by Foster Cline and Lisa Greene

Meeting the Challenge—Using Love and Logic to Help Children Develop Attention and Behavior Skills
by Jim Fay and Foster Cline

Cameron's Corner

"While I love to be in control of my own choices, sometimes without restrictions, I would be lost and not know what the correct choice or decision is without some rules or feedback."

9

Meltdowns Will Happen—Be Prepared

Why?

Children with ASD get tired and frustrated like any other child, but on a magnified scale. They quickly get overstimulated by the environment and frustrated by the fact the world isn't working as expected. It seriously hurts their feelings that everyone else doesn't see things the way they do. Meltdowns may come due to being overwhelmed or due to feelings of powerlessness. Expect the meltdowns. You will deal with them better if you have a plan in place for when they happen.

How?

- KEEP CALM!! (Easier said than done, but this had to be said.)

- Understand that when your child is having an explosion of emotion, there is always a root cause. A meltdown is a form of communication. The child can't get what he wants so he responds in the only way he knows. Examples of causes for meltdowns are: tiredness, sensory overload, lack of quality sleep, physical effects from troublesome foods, not getting wants, onset of illness, needing attention, hunger, feeling a lack of control over a situation, trying to test the rules in order to learn, not knowing what to do or what is expected in a situation, or frustration due to being unable to voice wants or needs.

- Take note of the times your child has extreme emotions most often and try to avoid these situations for now.

- Sometimes trying to figure out the cause of the meltdown at the moment it is occurring is difficult and takes more energy than you have. Instead, move your child to a quiet, safe place to give him time to calm down. Use soothing words and tell your child that everything is okay. This in itself may be all he needed in the first place.

- Look for body signals that a meltdown is coming on such as hands balled into fists, eyes squeezed shut, faster breathing, shaking, swaying or rocking, increased stimming, rapid blinking, or a clenched jaw. When you see these signals, take action immediately to find out what is distressing your child before he melts down.

- Try diversion tactics. Give him something out of his travel bag to play with or ask him to help you with something.

- Don't bribe or threaten your child when he is melting down. This will not help him learn how to calm himself, but will cause further frustration.

- When a child blows up, recognize his need to blow off steam due to stress that has built up. Help him find ways to blow off steam such as playful exercise.

- When your child is melting down, give him words to express how he may be feeling or what he is trying to say. Examples may be, "I know you are tired and want to go home," or, "I know you are angry that we are at the grocery store instead of the park." This will help him learn how to tell you what is wrong in the future. Again, emphasize that everything is going to be okay.

- When a meltdown is coming on say, "Use your words and tell me what you need." You may not get a response at first, but say it each time until he is able to voice his needs.

- Keep your language simple, as his stressed mind may not be able to process more complicated thoughts.

- Tell your child that crying when upset is a wonderful way for his body to get bad feelings out. But give him rules about that, too. A little crying to express himself is okay (maybe five minutes), but a thirty-minute crying tantrum is not.

- ☐ Don't automatically give in to what your child wants. If the meltdown is actually a tantrum is due to not getting things as he expected, use this as a learning opportunity or simply take him home. Giving in to a tantrum, by giving your child what he wants or expects, encourages him to communicate through tantrums in the future.

- ☐ Talk to your child about times he gets extremely frustrated. Tell him you understand his frustration. Everyone gets frustrated. Discuss a plan for what to do when this happens. Discuss a past frustration and talk your child through it with possible solutions. See the following page for an example discussion.

Out and About

- ☐ Don't worry about what others are thinking. Focus only on you, your child's safety, and the best way to calm the situation quickly—even if this means changing your plans.

- ☐ Have someone on call to come pick up your child if he is having a meltdown, but you can't leave, and take him to a quiet place. Save this option for emergencies.

- ☐ Create a backup plan if your child is too big to pick up and you can't get him to calm down. Do you have a male relative that could come help you out in a pinch?

Book Nook

Try and Make Me! Simple Strategies That Turn Off the Tantrums and Create Cooperation
by Ray Levy and Bill O'Hanlon

Let's Talk About It

We were at the store and six-year-old Cameron saw something he wanted. I said he couldn't have it. In his mind, he felt that since he wanted it, he should get it! When I said *no*, he threw himself down on to the floor of the store. He was crying, screaming and banging his head on the floor. In this situation, because nothing would calm him, I simply picked him up and carried him out of the store, past the adults saying, "Poor kid," and went home where "poor Mom" could breathe in relief and Cameron could calm down in his comfy spot.

Discussion after everything is calm:

Mom: What happened when I said you couldn't have the candy bar at the store?

Cam: I wanted the candy bar and there was no reason (for Mom to say no). I should have gotten the candy bar.

Mom: So you were frustrated that you couldn't have the candy bar? (I mirrored the emotion to Cameron)

Cam: (nods head) I wanted the candy bar.

Mom: (I tried to keep lesson short)
(1) The rule is, Cameron, that a lot of times people can't have what they want and they don't always know the reason. I may want a million dollars, but I won't be able to get it just because I want it.

(2) When you scream and yell and bang your head, I get scared that you will hurt yourself.

(3) Some people who get frustrated or angry, instead of yelling and banging their heads, try breathing deeply and thinking of something else, talking to someone about it, or going to a quiet place to be by themselves. Next time you can't get something you want, what would you like to choose to do? (I offered narrow choices)

Cam: I'll go by myself.

Try to use as few and as simple words as possible to solve the problem. One discussion most likely won't solve the problem. Repeat the discussion after the next meltdown, when things have calmed, and remind your child of better choices.

When he is at the beginning of a meltdown, remind your child, that there are better choices. In the heat of the moment, it may be difficult for him to remember without help. "Cameron, I see you are getting frustrated because you can't have a new ball. What will you choose to do?" If he doesn't respond with a choice, you can ask, "Do you need me to tell you the choices again?"

At School

☐ Talk to your child's teacher about possible meltdowns. Let him know that you are working on ways to understand the meltdowns and to help your child through them. Discuss what can be done in the classroom or other places in the school if your child has a meltdown. Safety for both your child and the other children is extremely important. If your child loses control of his emotions often, make this discussion a priority.

☐ Come up with a place your child can go at school if he has a meltdown outside of the classroom—perhaps the school office, or the nurse's or counselor's room. Make it understood that this is a chance for your child to get his body and mind to calm down.

☐ In the classroom, having a comfy spot is extremely important. This will help your child keep it together longer if he can get to the comfy spot to calm down before his body gets out of control.

Important Tip

The good news is, the part of your child's life where he completely melts down will not last forever! The more you connect with him, teach him to communicate, and help him overcome sensory overload, the better he will be able to handle the world around him. Also, remember that meltdowns are a form of communication. Praise your child for letting you know that he is upset.

At Other Homes

Hopefully, you have already worked out ahead of time a place for your child to go if he gets stressed out. If he starts to melt down, take him immediately to this place and help him calm down. Once he is calm, ask if he would like to stay in the quiet place for a little while until he feels better.

What Else?

Teach your child calm breathing by blowing bubbles together. This can be done outdoors or in the bathtub at bath time. Bubbles can be brought along on trips outside the home as a calming item.

Cameron's Corner

"There are times when things just have to be my way and I get very upset. An argument often follows. I go off into my own space to cool down. This helps me to reflect on the situation and compromise whenever possible."

Special Section—Teaching Safety

Because the child with ASD does not always understand social situations this makes him even more vulnerable in situations that could be unsafe. Do everything you can to teach him ways to keep himself safe.

Body Safety

Tell him that no one should be touching his naked body except his doctor and his caretaker during a bath. Talk about what privates mean and again that no one should be touching those except his doctor sometimes and during a bath. Remind him that if anyone else tries to touch him like this that he should tell you right away.

Teach your child a phrase he can use that means, "Don't touch me!"

Know The Code

Create a code word for your family to use if you need someone to pick your children up in an emergency. Teach your children that if a person tries to get them to go somewhere with him and he doesn't know the code, **Don't Go**!

Important Tip

Always encourage your child to talk to you about anything and everything. If your child brings up something he did that he shouldn't have, instead of getting angry or judging, discuss the situation and the possible consequences. Allow your child to talk to you about subjects that may seem mature. Talk to him on his level about the topic. If you don't know how, get help from someone with more experience. The more you talk to your child, the more he will feel comfortable coming to you right away if something bad or dangerous happens.

What Is A Stranger?

In our home, we use the green light, yellow light and red light system for how to tell who to trust. It goes like this:

Green Light People: These are people Mom and Dad have named who can be trusted. In fact, they can be trusted so much that if they show up at school to pick up your child and you haven't told them ahead of time, your child should trust them enough to go with them. This list should be small (about 10 people) and is usually family, closest friends, most trusted people from church, etc. Write out a list of these people and go over it often.

Yellow Light People: These are people that we are not 100% sure about so, just to be safe, your child can talk to them only if you are around or if they ask you first. Your child should not talk to these people if he sees them when no other adult is around and he should never go anywhere with these people unless you have specifically told him it is okay. This list could also include complete strangers, but your child is standing with you or a trusted adult at the time of the conversation.

Red Light People: Don't trust them, don't talk to them, and don't go anywhere with them **ever**! These would be complete strangers when your child has no trusted adult with him. These can also be any people you want to name that you feel are unsafe for your child in any situation.

Tattling

Here is a simple rule for telling on someone else. If a child is causing harm or may cause harm to himself or others, **tell**!

If your child just can't help himself and he feels the need to tattle to the teacher whenever someone breaks a rule, have him write them all down instead. He can give a daily report to the teacher in writing at the end of the day and she can decide whether to act on any of the tattles.

Peer Pressure

- ☐ Talk about how other kids may try to pressure your child into doing things he shouldn't do or things he doesn't want to do. There are many reasons for this, but the reasons aren't important. What is important is helping your child know when to say *no*.

- ☐ Teach this rule: Always say *no* when what you are being asked to do is against the law or against the rules.

- ☐ Teach this rule: Be suspicious when you are not sure if what you are being asked will get you into trouble or if the person asking has gotten you into trouble before.

- ☐ Teach your child how to use the green light, yellow light, red light method for peers.

- ☐ Tell your child that friends often ask you to keep secrets, but secrets should never be kept if they affect someone's safety.

- ☐ Always encourage your child to talk to you about his day and to ask you about any situations that come up if he isn't sure how to handle them.

Book Nook

Don't Talk to Strangers, Pooh (picture book)
by Kathleen W. Zoehfeld

Your Body Belongs to You (picture book)
by Cornelia M. Spelman
(about body safety)

Special Section—Girls With Autism Spectrum Disorder

For every five children diagnosed with ASD, four are boys and one is a girl. Although all the same techniques apply, there may be some special considerations for girls. I suggest reading the following books on the subject from these excellent authors:

(1) **Aspergers and Girls**
Featuring Tony Atwood, Temple Grandin, and more

(2) **Safety Skills for Asperger Women**
by Liane Holliday Willey

(3) **Girls Growing Up on the Spectrum—What Parents and Professionals Should Know About Preteen and Teenage Years**
by Shana Nichols

(4) **The Care and Keeping of You—The Body Book for Younger Girls**
by Victoria Schaefer (An American Girls Book)

Or

(5) **The Care and Keeping of You 2—The Body Book for Older Girls**
by Cara Natterson (An American Girls Book)

Special Section—Guest Parent Post

My name is Jenny-Lee and I have three children with ASD. I have watched them struggle to interact, I've been deafened by elective mutism, I've been on the receiving end of violent outbursts, seen numerous meltdowns, watched them bounce for endless hours on yoga balls, I've cried, laughed and pulled at my hair in frustration. So here are some things I have learned along the way over the last 21 years.

1. **Every moment is a teaching moment.** You may need to think hard about it, but there is always a lesson that can be learned in every situation.
2. **Keep your routines short and simple.** Go slow. He needs simple instructions so he can learn confidently. Give one instruction at a time.
3. **Use visual aid cards wherever possible.** (I use Board Maker to create my own. There are other programs available as well.) These give your child a sense of independence.
4. **Be positive.** When you role model positive language and behaviour, your child will learn how to do the same. It also helps your emotional wellbeing.
5. **Teach him about personal safety.** Everyone needs to learn about personal safety, and your child is no exception. Use Social Stories (like *Everyone's Got a Bottom* by Tess Rowley) to teach him about self-protection.
6. **Have safe zones and encourage him to use them** when he feels overwhelmed. My son has designated safe zones (sand pit, veggie garden, and his room). It took about a year for him to learn how to use them consistently, and I nearly gave up, until one day he said to me, "Mommy, I'm feeling like I'm losing my plot. I'm going to my safe zone for a calm down time." This one moment was worth every tear I shed and every second I spent teaching him to use his safe zone.
7. **Sensory Bags.** These can contain all the things that you know soothe your child. We keep them with us or in the car ready to use just like a first aid kit. Ours have: a water bottle or sippy cup, a neck pillow, light travel blanket, colouring sheets and pencils, some preferred snack foods, a music device and

headphones, basic visual aid cards on a lanyard for out and about, stress ball or slime (every child has a preference), a sensory toy of choice (we made our own glitter bottles), and a favourite storybook. You can put in it whatever is appropriate for your child. Having a sensory bag is like giving him a toolbox. When he's feeling overwhelmed or about to lose control, he can open the bag and use whatever he needs in order to regulate himself again. This is also a great way for him to learn about self-regulation and emotional input.

8. **Yoga Balls are fun and affordable.** Does your child fidget? Does he get up and down constantly and end up so sidetracked he forgets what he's doing, even eating his dinner? Well, my youngest daughter was this way. She has Hyperactivity Disorder and Gut Dysbiosis, along with her ASD, so she is always fidgeting. A specialist therapist, who was actually working with my son, suggested replacing her chair with a yoga ball. I did, figuring why not at least try, and to my surprise, my daughter ate all her dinner. She bounced and rocked and twirled nonstop, but she didn't leave the table until she had finished.

9. **Journaling.** This has been a blessing for me. It's a great way to vent without shouting. I encourage everyone to try it at least once.

10. **Going Natural.** While there are exceptions, I always try to use natural therapies and remedies with my children. When they have a cold, I use my mother's recipe of honey, lemon, and hot water to ease symptoms. We drink chamomile for stress and anxiety (can also be added to the bath). Turmeric can be added to pancake mixture (or nearly any cooking) and is a natural anti-inflammatory. Ginger is great for nausea and travel sickness. Speak to a naturopath if you are interested in going natural. They can offer a lot of invaluable insight.

11. **Arts and Crafts.** I pull out the butcher's paper and an assortment of pens, crayons, chalks, paints, and charcoals and my children come running! Making pom poms or crocheting a beanie—it doesn't matter what sort of arts and crafts you do, this is valuable time you and your child can spend together making memories. Get yourself in there and get creative. It will help you to bond with them.

12. **Clocks.** Sometimes children get up and wander the house when everyone is sleeping. My eldest daughter used to and when I asked her doctor about it, she told me to put a ticking clock in her bedroom because the ticking sounds act as a comforter. It actually worked.

13. **Just Enjoy Now.** I know it's hard, but try to see three good things in every day,

laugh at his attempts to humour you, and always tell him you are proud of his efforts. The good days and the bad days, the funny and the sad ones, enjoy them all. And remember, it's okay to smile.

14. **Friendships Matter.** We all want to have friends who love and accept us. Children with ASD want that as well, the same as anyone else does. Try to be supportive of their friendship choices, even if they are not ones you agree with.

> "This is our reality. I am awed and inspired by my children's courage and determination every day."
> **Jenny-Lee on parenting ASD children**

A Few Quirky Tips by Jenny-Lee

- Need to soften clothes and linens, but fabric softener makes your child upset? Try adding 1/2 cup of vinegar to the last rinse cycle instead. It doesn't leave any odours, kills mildew, and softens.
- Does your child hate veggies? Try grinding them up and adding them to meat sauces like Spaghetti Bolognese. They will become invisible.
- Savoury muffins are great for lunch instead of sandwiches and you can freeze them for up to three months.
- Does your child eat play-dough? Make your own at home and add natural colours. At least when he eats it, you will know it had no harsh chemicals or preservatives that could be harmful.
- A handmade knitted or crocheted blanket has the same effect as a weighted blanket if it's made from a heavier wool, and it is more affordable. But make sure the blanket ends are tied correctly for safety. You can put a blanket cover over the knitted or crocheted blanket to help add another layer of safety.
- A neck pillow (travel pillow) is a great sensory tool for kids with ASD. A water bottle that requires they suck on the top to get liquid out is as well. This stimulates and massages the muscles in the mouth and neck which helps promote a sense of being safe.
- Do you get pen and marker drawings all over the wall? Tape up large sheets of butcher's paper everywhere your child gets creative and let him go for it. Keep the sheets and use them as a fun homemade wrapping paper for gifts.
- Do you need help cleaning those art works off the wall? Cheap hairspray, a cloth, and hot water works a treat for most surprise artwork. Spray the hairspray over the drawing 2-3 cm's (about an inch) and count to thirty. Wring out the wet cloth and firmly wash the area.

Special Section—Sleep

Many children with ASD have trouble with sleep. For some of them, this is the result of a body that is still feeling overstimulated even once they have gone to bed in a dark quiet room. Here are a few tips to help sleep come a little easier.

- Make sure there is little stimulation an hour before bed. We call this *quiet time* in our home. Turn off all electronic devices and play quiet music.

- Create a soothing bedtime routine that ends with children having their own quiet time in their rooms before sleeping. This can include reading or quiet play.

- If your child prefers, make his room completely dark with no night light and a closed door. Get blackout curtains or blinds if this helps.

- Get a sound machine to block out outdoor noises or noises coming from other parts of the house.

- If possible, allow your ASD child not to share a bedroom.

- ☐ Check to see if your child's diet is causing digestive discomfort which can make sleep difficult.

- ☐ If your child likes pressure, consider bedtime massage or some sort of pressure such as a weighted blanket before bed. **For safety, be sure that any weighted items are the correct weight for your child. Work With an expert to determine this.**

- ☐ When you are going away from home, don't forget your child's favorite blanket, pillow, and stuffed animal to help him sleep better.

Consult your child's doctor or natural healthcare provider before considering the following:

- ☐ Consider herbal tea for sleep such as chamomile.

- ☐ Consider giving your child melatonin (Use caution! This is a hormone and can affect growth if not used properly.)

- ☐ If a sleeping problem persists, consult with your child's doctor or natural healthcare provider for further suggestions.

SCHOOL

If you haven't already done so, ask for a meeting with your child's school principal, her teacher, and the special education coordinator or school counselor.

Why?

No matter what level your child is at educationally, she will require some accommodations in the classroom and during social activities. It is best to have a team approach where you can discuss your child's difficulties and needs. Having the stigma of being in a special education program may seem difficult at first, but it will open doors to additional help for your child that would not be open otherwise. **Weigh the pros and cons and decide if the help is worth that label for your child.**

IEP or 504?

In order to get the accommodations (help) your child needs, she must be on an IEP (Individual Education Plan) or a 504 plan (a plan for accommodations for those children with a medical diagnosis, but who do not otherwise need specialized instruction). An IEP is a written document that states what your child is having difficulty with, how these difficulties were proven (tests, observation), and what is going to be done to achieve the goals laid out in the plan. The goals do not have to be academic in nature. These can include things such as joining in, staying in the room, interacting with others, communication. Difficulties in areas other than academics can hinder the overall learning process. Therefore, a child with ASD, no matter how far ahead she may be academically, qualifies for help. The IEP or 504 is helpful to you because whatever goals are written there, the school **must** work towards helping your child to achieve them. Without the written document, the school may not help you to its best ability.

Although there are federal special education laws, every state and every school district has its own rules. You can search your school district's or state department of education's website for *special education rights* or call the state department asking for a written copy of the rights. They are required to provide them for you. It is in your child's best interest to learn what your school district and your state are **required** to provide for your child. You will also need to make sure you can prove your child's disability through the measurements your state requires. If the correct measurement (test) hasn't been done, find out if the school is required to perform this for your child at their cost.

If someone says *no* to you when asking for a test or an accommodation for your child, get a second opinion. Make sure they are saying no because they are not required to do it rather than because they don't want to do it. If they say no to a test, find out if there is a state agency that will provide it for free or low cost.

The Meeting

- ☐ Your child has been diagnosed with ASD, you need to meet with a team of people at school. This usually includes the teacher, the special education coordinator, the school counselor and often the principal, the person who completed the testing, and any other specialists the school provides such as speech or occupational therapists. It is best to have more people at the initial meeting so everyone knows what the difficulties are, what the tests say, and what goals will be created.

- ☐ Before this meeting, visit your child's classroom and spend some time observing what happens there and how your child reacts and interacts with the classroom environment. This will give you more information when setting goals. What you see at home may very well not be what happens at school.

- ☐ Come prepared with a list of your child's difficulties including learning and social. Also, make a list of goals. What would you like to see your child accomplish during the school year? Keep the list simple. Remember that the school has guidelines they must work within and may not be able to help your child with all the goals no matter how worthy they are.

- Consider bringing a friend or other family member as an advocate. This person can be there to take notes about the meeting and to ask questions. It helps immensely to have an extra pair of eyes and ears especially when this can be a very emotional event for you, the parent. It can also help to keep you as the leading person in the room. Occasionally, schools will not offer all services available to a parent if they feel they can get it past you. They are usually working with minimal staff and budgets. But don't be afraid to stand up for your child and say, "Aren't you required to provide this for my child?" If they say *no*, let them know you will be checking on that with the school district before taking that as the final answer.

- **Do not** sign the IEP or 504 plan if you are not satisfied that it is written to the best advantage of your child. If it does not include enough help or is inappropriate for your child then it should not be put into practice. Your signing is your approval, and it will then be carried out to the letter—nothing more and nothing less.

- **Do not** be afraid to ask for multiple meetings or to ask around for more information. The first IEP or 504 plan is the most important, as it will set the stage for future years. Get everything on the plan that you can now. Accommodations can always be removed later as they become unnecessary.

- Be very careful of anyone who offers advocate services for pay. They often charge very high prices for services you can accomplish on your own. They may offer to work with the school for you to get services. Many areas have programs that provide **free** advocacy for you. If they cannot provide someone to come with you to meetings, it may be helpful to call and get advice on what your state is required to provide for your child. These centers are often the best places to find information since they keep current on the changing laws regarding services provided to children with disabilities. To find an autism advocacy group in your state, check with your school district or simply search on the internet and begin making a few calls. You will eventually get steered in the right direction. If the first call is unhelpful, try someone else. Help is available.

What Else?

☐ If your child does very well academically, you may ask yourself, *Why should she be labeled as having a disability and be put on an education plan?* The answer is, because there are many areas she needs help in that affect her daily life and may continue to do so without intervention. She may be very strong in math, but struggling with reading. She may have difficulty staying in the classroom and withstanding the constant sensory input. She may have visual difficulties that are making it hard for her to get through the day without feeling wiped out. One problem might be something she could withstand, but begin stacking all of your child's challenges on top of each other and you can see how much harder she has to work to accomplish learning. The school is required to help your child work at her level. With this stack of difficulties on top of her, is she really working to the best of her abilities?

☐ **Insist that social skills be placed on the IEP.** This is crucial as this may be the most important skill needed to help her succeed.

☐ Don't forget to ask for some of the following accommodations if they would be helpful to your child: Preferred seating, extra time to complete work, a quiet place to work, oral assignments instead of written, using the computer to complete assignments, or any accommodations that will help calm sensory issues.

☐ Ask that the school provide your child with a contact person in the classroom or the school for times when she has questions or concerns. This person should be available at regular and predictable times for your child whether it is an hourly, daily, or weekly check-in.

☐ At the beginning of each school year, ask for permission to tour the school before it is in session. This will allow your child to walk the halls and see her new classroom and hopefully the new teacher before all the extra sensory input comes. This will help calm her fears.

- ☐ Check in with your child regularly to confirm that she is receiving the services that were listed on her IEP.

- ☐ Discuss with the school ways in which you can ensure that your child will never be unsupervised before school, after school, and during other vulnerable times. This will protect her from situations in which she doesn't know what to do to keep herself safe.

If All Else Fails?

If you feel it is the most appropriate starting place for you and your child, look into the option of homeschooling. While you are beginning this journey of help and healing for your child, this may be the best option. If you do homeschool, consider how you will later transition your child into a group setting for her benefit.

Important Tip

Remember, you are your child's advocate. Don't be afraid to stand up on her behalf. I often use the phrase, "The squeaky wheel gets the grease." For your child's sake, be as squeaky as you feel you need to be! On the flip side, don't forget to respect the hard work teachers put into their jobs and the rules and laws that may hinder them from doing all that could possibly be done.

Book Nook

The Everyday Advocate—Standing Up for Your Child with Autism
by Areva Martin

Simple Strategies That Work—Helpful Hints for All Educators of Students with Asperger Syndrome, High Functioning Autism and Related Disabilities
by Brenda Smith Myles with Diane Adreon and Dena Gitlitz
(A short book with simple strategies for **educators**)

Homeschooling the Child With Asperger Syndrome
by Lise Pyles

A Parent's Guide to Special Education: Insider Advice on How to Navigate the System and Help Your Child Succeed
Linda Wilmshurst and Alan W. Brue
(Provides help understanding the IEP and special education)

DIET

Why Consider Your Child's Diet?

There are many reasons to take a long hard look at your child's diet. First, your child is under heavy stress. This stress can be hard on the body. A good healthy diet will help keep the body stronger in times of stress. Second, many parents of children on the spectrum have found their children have digestive issues and have seen great improvement in behavior and mood with positive diet changes. Talk to your child's doctor, a nutrition specialist, or a natural healthcare provider before making any major diet changes if you need guidance.

- ☐ Consider a whole foods diet free of processed foods—including fast food. Processed foods are generally low in nutritional value and harder for the body to digest.

- ☐ Limit sugar intake. Again, the body has to work harder to process high amounts of sugar and it contains little to no nutritional value. For a slightly higher nutritional value, consider raw forms of sugar such as raw honey, real maple syrup, and raw sugar.

- ☐ Consider a good multivitamin to support your child's extra nutritional needs. Choose a multivitamin that does not contain added sugars, fillers, preservatives, and food coloring. Always check the ingredients to see what has been added. Often, you have to pay a little bit more for a higher quality product.

- ☐ Consider food allergy testing. Many children with ASD have been found to test positive for food allergies—especially dairy and gluten. When a child is eating foods that upset the digestion you may see an increase in difficult behaviors and distress. Ask for a blood test rather than a scratch test for the food allergies, as it is a better measurement and less stressful to the child.

- ☐ You will hear a lot about a GFCF (gluten free/casein free) diet. This is an elimination of all dairy and foods with gluten such as wheat, rye, and barley. I would recommend food allergy testing first so you have a definite measurement of what may be causing digestive upset. In our case, Cameron's tests came back positive for allergies to dairy, gluten, soy, eggs, peanuts, shellfish and more. This was more of a challenge at first than expected, but worth every moment to make the changes. Work with a nutritionist who is familiar with food allergies or a natural healthcare provider who can help guide you in how to eliminate foods properly. If you do not want to go this route right away or the cost is too much, try going gluten free and dairy free for at least a month. It takes this long to get the allergens out of the system. See if your child improves. Do not be surprised if he is cranky at first or has an increase in symptoms. This often happens when first detoxing an allergen from the body and should go away within 2-3 weeks.

- ☐ Carry small snacks with you for your child when you will be away from home. This way you can be sure to have a healthy choice available and be able to calm any stress brought on by hunger.

Important Tip

We have encountered many medical doctors who will not discuss nutrition or food allergies with us. I have been cut off when bringing it up or treated as an irrational mother. I stopped going to medical doctors for nutrition and diet support. Our family now works with a naturopathic clinic who has an onsite nutritionist. If you run into problems when trying to discuss diet and nutritional health with your child's MD, consider finding someone in the field of naturopathic medicine or a licensed nutritionist to help you.

Book Nook

The Kid-Friendly ADHD and Autism Cookbook: The Ultimate Guide to the Gluten-Free Casein-Free Diet
by Pamela Compart, Dana Laake, Jon B. Pangborn, and Sidney MacDonald Baker

Special Diets for Special Kids (volume 1 and 2)
by Lisa Lewis
(gluten-free, casein-free information with recipes)

Eating For Autism—The 10 step Nutrition Plan to Help Treat Your Child's Autism, Asperger's, or ADHD
by Elizabeth Strickland

www.gfcfdiet.com
("Autism diet"— For more information and Frequently Asked Questions)

SOCIAL TIME

This will probably be the greatest challenge in your home, and for this reason, it is especially important to start slowly and to not push your child to make social connections. It is best to begin by having absolutely no expectations in this area. If you push your child, you may meet with forceful resistance and may cause him to shrink back instead of moving forward. In the Next Steps section, you will find tips on how to build social behaviors. For now, simply let your child sit back and watch.

What To Do

- ☐ Be aware that in most cases, children with ASD truly want to socialize, but avoid it because of distress, fears or a simple lack of knowledge. This desire is a great place to begin.

- ☐ For now, don't make play dates or expect your child to be around groups of people often. If he does need to be in a group (such as a family gathering) allow him to sit on the sidelines by himself. Occasionally connect with him by asking how he is doing or if he needs anything. If your child seems to ignore you, don't worry. This is only the beginning.

- ☐ Occasionally bring your child's attention to what someone else is doing by pointing out, "Look at what Ben is doing. He is playing with his truck." Make sure your child acknowledges you in some small way even if it is shrugging you off. If you don't at first get his attention, try gently laying your hand on his head or shoulder and repeat what you said. Even if your child responds negatively to you, he has still made a very small connection in a social setting.

- ☐ If you bring your child somewhere where he is expected to participate (such as a swim party) and he doesn't wish to, tell him he can watch instead. Watching others in a social setting is an excellent way to learn social rules. Do not be discouraged that he is playing by himself.

- ☐ Teach your child about the body space bubble. Tell him that everyone has a space bubble about the size of arm's length around them. Many people do not like others in their space bubble without permission. If your child tends to crowd others, remind him that this puts him in their space bubbles. Let him tell others the same thing if he is uncomfortable having people close to him.

- ☐ Crowds are especially difficult places and easily cause sensory overload. Consider leaving your child at home or with a trusted babysitter when you expect to go somewhere with crowds such as the mall, restaurants, or indoor sports and entertainment events.

- ☐ Teach your child the appropriate voice levels using either a green light, yellow light, red light system or a number system where 5 is the loudest and 0 is silent. When your child is using the wrong voice level, remind him of which level he should be using. When going somewhere new, tell him "The rule is…" and what level his voice should be while there.

- ☐ If you send your child to a quiet corner, he will probably be extremely relieved, so time-out for a social mistake will not help him learn from that mistake. If your child does something wrong in a social setting, remember that he probably didn't know it was wrong and use this as an opportunity to teach or reteach the rules of the situation.

EXERCISE

Why?

Some exercise in some form is good for everyone. It leads the body to optimal health and alleviates stress. The ASD child is under a lot of stress. This stress and staying home in her own world most of the time will tighten up her muscles. Exercise will loosen up muscles and provide physical and emotional relief. Many children with ASD have motor skill difficulties. Exercise will help build these skills.

What?

- ☐ Don't expect organized exercise yet. Any movement will do. Take your child to the park to run around or use the play equipment. If she prefers the same playground toy every time, let her stay with it. Take short walks at a favorite place, walk the dog or go swimming. Find anything active she likes to do.

- ☐ If your child is resistant to outdoor play, get a little extra walking in by parking farther out in parking lots or taking the stairs in buildings. This will be good for you too!

- ☐ Many kids with ASD benefit from using a mini trampoline. Show her different ways of jumping on it. Be sure she is safe at all times. Put the trampoline where you can keep an eye on her activity. This can be used inside or outdoors.

- ☐ Teach slow breathing techniques. The best way to teach this is to have her lay on her back and place a light item like a stuffed animal on her belly. Show her how to breathe in such a way that the toy moves up and down with each breath. Let her choose the toy each time. Use a quiet voice during this time. Tell her that when she gets frustrated and doesn't know what to do, she can remember to do her slow breathing to calm down.

- ☐ Toss soft objects within the house such as bean bags, Koosh balls, Nerf balls or balloons. Remind your child that only soft objects can be thrown inside the house.

- ☐ Roll a ball back and forth on the floor.

- ☐ Make a target and let your child throw a soft item at it.

- ☐ Unless your child loves and thrives on sports, don't expect her to be on any teams right now.

- ☐ If you have a dog, let your child become the dog walker or let her hold the leash while you take the dog out.

- ☐ Make sure your child gets a small amount of on purpose physical activity (at least 10-15 minutes) outside of school every day.

- ☐ Take your child out in the sunlight for at least a few minutes every day when possible.

- ☐ Make sure the clothes your child is wearing during exercise and PE at school are comfortable and allow for ease of movement.

Book Nook

Brain Gym: Simple Activities for Whole Brain Learning
by Paul & Gail Dennison
(integrating learning through motion)

Smart Moves—Why Learning is Not All in Your Head
by Carla Hannaford
(presents the body's role in thinking and learning)

"There are no secrets to success. It is the result of preparation, hard work, and learning from failure."

—Colin Powell

NEXT STEPS

Now it is time to dig in! You have learned what upsets your child the most and what calms him. You've taken note of his most troublesome issues. You have probably talked to a few experts including school staff. The next step is to begin making connections, teaching new skills, and trying out interventions. Complete each activity in the "Role-Play" boxes in this section to help you accomplish these goals.

This will be the most difficult stage. There may be a few days when both you and your child are crying in frustration. Consider these growing pains. If you want your child to grow and learn, you will have to make him uncomfortable at times. Just keep envisioning reaching your goals and remember that it will get better with time. So let's get to work!

1

Learn All You Can About The Helpful Stuff

Why?

No one has all the answers. Your child is unique and has many layers to his personality. Getting as many tools in your parenting toolbox is a win-win for you and your family.

How?

- ☐ Focus on information about what can help children with ASD. Steer clear of books and blogs that spend time on the negative or complain about symptoms. Don't weigh yourself down with information that is not helpful.

- ☐ Be skeptical of anyone who says they have the cure or the one thing that will make everything better. Healing is a journey. Each of your child's layers may require different kinds of attention.

- ☐ Thoroughly research any interventions before starting. See if you can find others to talk to who found each intervention helpful.

- ☐ Join an autism support group. Expect the tone of the group to be positive and helpful.

- ☐ Create a personal treatment plan for your family. List your child's strengths and weaknesses. Choose two or three goals you would like your child to achieve first. What is most important to his success? List techniques you would like to try or learn more about. List your resources—people who can help you on this journey. Schedule play time every day during which you will implement new strategies. Keep track of which interventions help and which ones don't. Don't immediately assume that an intervention not working now won't work later when your child may be ready for it.

- ☐ If your child does not respond as well to instruction from you, consider a play time trade with friends or family members a few times a week. Ask them to implement some of the strategies on your plan.

- ☐ Consider a mentor for your child. Find someone who understands his difficulties and is willing to help him learn to navigate the social world through fun activities.

- ☐ Find out what resources are available in your area specifically for autism. Ask your child's doctor or his school, or search the internet for possibilities.

- ☐ Learn all you can, but be careful of what the experts are telling you. Don't automatically assume what teach is going to succeed with your child. Always get more than one opinion if you can and weigh those against what you know about your child.

- ☐ Be careful of internet information. A lot of people have a lot to say and it's not always accurate or helpful.

- ☐ Ask other parents about what has helped their children. If you see a positive trend, consider trying out the idea.

- ☐ Don't be afraid to take advantage of free resources. They may lead you further in the direction you wish to go.

Important Tip

Don't forget to take time for yourself. Go out as a couple when you can or schedule at least an hour a week to do something just for you. You will be of more help to your whole family if you take the time to recharge your batteries. Don't be afraid to seek counseling as well if this will help lighten your burden. And remember to pray for help and wisdom.

Cameron's Corner

"I didn't use to like talking about my ASD. I saw it as a hindrance to me. But now, I realize understanding more about it encourages me to be proud of my accomplishments. I like to talk to people who are related to others with ASD to give them insight and help."

Book Nook

 ## Books on Autism and Asperger's

The Asperger's Answer Book—The Top 300 Questions Parents Ask
by Susan Ashley

The Complete Guide to Asperger's Syndrome
by Tony Atwood

The Oasis Guide to Asperger Syndrome—Advice, Support, Insight, and Inspiration
by Patricia Romanowski Bashe, Barbara L. Kirby, and Tony Attwood
(comprehensive overview)

The Way I See It—A Personal Look at Autism and Asperger's
by Temple Grandin
(good basic overview)

Autism Spectrum Disorders—The Complete Guide to Understanding Autism, Asperger's Syndrome, Pervasive Developmental Disorder and Other ASDs
by Chantal Sicile-Kira

 ## Stories by Parents & Personal Accounts

The Spark—A Mother's Story of Nurturing Genius
by Kristine Barnett
(A mother's story of how she ignored the experts who said her child couldn't learn and instead listened to intuition to give her son a happy and healthy life.)

Not My Boy
by Rodney Peete
("A father, a son and one family's journey with autism")

Be Different—Adventures of a Free-Range Aspergian—With Practical Advice for Aspergians, Misfits, Families and Teachers
by John Elder Robison
("He describes growing up with Asperger's syndrome at a time when the diagnosis didn't exist" funny and intelligent)

The Boy Who Loved Windows: Opening the Heart and Mind of a Child Threatened with Autism
by Patricia Stacey
(A mother's story of using the Floortime Approach to change her son's life.)

Pretending to be Normal—Living with Asperger's Syndrome
by Liane Holliday Willey

Asperger Syndrome in the Family—Redefining Normal
by Liane Holliday Willey

❋ Parenting Books

Boundaries with Kids
by Henry Cloud & John Townsend
(How to help children establish healthy boundaries for maturity and to learn responsibility. How to set limits in a loving way.)

Pick Up Your Socks and Other Skills Growing Children Need: A Practical Guide to Raising Responsible Children
by Elizabeth Crary

Peaceful Parents, Peaceful Kids
by Naomi Drew
(17 simple keys to peaceful parenting. Formatted in an easy way to accomplish one key idea at a time.)

Positive Discipline for Children with Special Needs—Raising and Teaching all Children to Become Resilient, Responsible and Respectful
by Jane Nelson, Steven Foster and Arlene Raphael
(A bit more clinical, but very good approaches. There is a complete series of positive discipline books.)

How to Behave so Your Children Will, Too!
by Sal Severe

How to Behave so Your Preschooler Will, Too!
by Sal Severe

Simplify Your Life With Kids: 100 Ways to Make Family Life Easier and More Fun
by Elaine St. James

No: Why Kids of All Ages Need to Hear it and Ways Parents Can Say it
by David Walsh

✳ Intervention Ideas

Asperger Syndrome and Young children—Building Skills for the Real World—For People Who Know and Care for 3-7 Year Olds
by Teresa Bolick
(a little clinical but good ideas)

Apps for Autism—An Essential Guide to Over 200 Effective Apps for Improving Communication, Behavior, Social Skills, and More
by Lois Jean Brady

The Mislabeled Child—Looking Beyond Behavior to Find the True Sources and Solutions for Children's Learning Challenges
by Brock Eide & Fernette Eide

Quirky, Yes—Hopeless, No: Practical Tips to Help Your Child With Asperger's Syndrome Be More Socially Accepted
by Cynthia LaBrie Norall and Beth Wagner Brust
(85 lessons for decoding children with Asperger's.)

1001 Great Ideas for Teaching and Raising Children with Autism Spectrum Disorders
by Ellen Notbohm & Veronica Zysk

Finding Your Way—Practical Solutions for Creating a Supportive Home and Community for the Asperger Syndrome Family
by Kristi Sakai
(taking care of your child, taking care of yourself, community support)

I Can Problem Solve (ICPS) (Kindergarten & Primary)
I Can Problem Solve (ICPS) (Intermediate Elementary)
Raising a Thinking Child
Raising a Thinking Preteen: I Can Problem Solve 8-12 Year Olds
Thinking Parent, Thinking Child
all by Myrna Shure

Cutting Edge Therapies for Autism
by Ken Siri & Tony Lyons

❋ Websites

www.autismspeaks.org
("One of the leading autism science and advocacy organizations")

www.aspergersyndrome.org
(OASIS@MAAP (now called Autism Spectrum Coalition—a resource for parents of those on the autism spectrum)

www.autism.com
(Autism Research Institute—learn about autism and Asperger's and treatments)

www.autismnow.org
(The National Autism Resource and Information Center provides resources and information for individuals with ASD and other developmental disabilities)

www.freespirit.com
(free spirit publishing—great books for kids)

www.learning-styles-online.com
(to learn more about learning styles)

www.tacanow.org
(Talk about Curing Autism Now—has information and resources)

2

Begin Moving Your Child Out Of Her Comfort Zone

Why?

Your child's comfy spot will not always be available. She will need to learn how to comfort herself in tough situations.

How?

- ☐ Begin by creating a comfy spot in a family room where you spend the most time together. Let your child put some of her favorite things there.

- ☐ Continue to allow your child to bring a comfort item wherever she goes. This is her connection to a feeling of safety and comfort.

- ☐ Encourage your child to come out of her comfy spot or room more often. Even if she is merely doing her own thing while everyone else is doing something different, this will help her to make connections.

- ☐ Little by little, increase the time your child is out and about. Set a goal. Start with a very small goal. Then add a few minutes at a time until you reach your goal. Once the goal is reached, set a new goal and work towards it.

- ☐ Begin bringing your child with you to the places where you normally wouldn't. Keep the time there short. Let your child simply become familiar with these places.

- ☐ When your child gets stressed and overstimulated try to distract her. First, remind her to take a deep breath and then ask her about something else or ask her to help you with what you are doing. This will encourage her to stay present longer. If these strategies don't work, then let her go to her comfy spot.

☐ If your child is a visual person, teach her to visualize her comfy spot in her mind so when she is out and about she can think about it, pretend she is there, and use this to calm herself.

Role-Play!

Begin role-playing possible difficult situations. For example: "Nicole, we are going to the park. What would you do if your favorite swing has been taken away and replaced by a slide?" She may try to deny this is a possibility and she may get upset. Remind her to take a deep breath and tell her you are just playing *what if*. If she won't answer the question you can offer choices like this: "If my favorite toy was taken away, here is what I might choose to do. 1) Play with something else, 2) Find out if another park has swings, 3) Go somewhere else and not play at the park at all."

Important Tip

Remember, during the First Steps, it was important to keep your child calm. But, in order to build connections and help your child move forward towards success, you will need to make her feel uncomfortable at times. Now is the time to begin. Be sure to move in small steps and give your child plenty of comfort and encouragement along the way. You don't want your child to become so uncomfortable that she melts down. Watch for signs that tell you it may be time to take a break.

Cameron's Corner

"I had to be pushed to do things out of my comfort zone at first. Eventually, I began doing new things by myself."

Special Section—Play Time

Of all the things you do for your child, play will be at the top of the importance list. Nothing helps a child connect like play time! Usually, children learn from other children during play time. They make connections, solve problems by acting things out, use their imagination, learn social rules, and build a sense of self. For the ASD child, however, you may have to work a little harder and in a particular manner to make those connections happen.

This is where the DIR®Floortime™ Technique can help. DIR stands for Developmental, Individual Difference, Relationship. The objectives of the floortime technique are to build healthy social, emotional, and intellectual abilities rather than focusing on skills and isolated behaviors."

I am recommending this as a must-have tool in your toolbox. When I read about this technique, I realized this is what I had instinctively done with my son due in part to my training as an elementary school teacher. So, from experience, I can tell you this method works. It not only works for children with ASD, but can build healthy skills for all children.

So what is the DIR®Floortime™ method? It is a method of play in which you connect with your child by meeting him where he is at. There are two goals to DIR®Floortime™. One is, to follow your child's lead, and the second is, to bring your child into a shared world. As parents with ASD children, this is our ultimate goal.

I highly recommend reading the books from the Book Nook in this section and going to the DIR®Floortime™ website to learn about this technique, how to implement it, and how to get help using it in your home. This technique can require a lot of time, energy, and persistence, but it is worth every moment of the effort as you watch your child grow.

Don't forget, however, that every child is different. Every child learns at a different speed and responds differently. Even Dr. Greenspan, creator of the DIR®Floortime™ approach, would tell you that it is one part of a multi-disciplinary approach. In other words, floortime alone will not heal your child. It is merely one piece of the puzzle—albeit a very large piece.

Here are some play time techniques to help you get started based on what I have learned from my own experiences:

- ☐ Start by getting down on the floor with your child or joining him where he is playing.

- ☐ Use one toy of focus at a time. If your child is playing with a favorite toy, you can bring in a toy of your own to interact with his toy, but no more. More toys create distraction.

- ☐ Look for clues that your child is getting tired and shutting down. Stop play time when your child has had enough. This does not mean stop because he is irritated. Look for physical signs of exhaustion.

- When possible, get in your child's face. In other words, so close that he can't help but see you.

- **Do not force eye contact.** Your job is to make yourself so exciting that he can't help but look at you.

- Use a very animated tone of voice. You know—the kind you see people use when talking to babies. "How cute you are! Oh, yes you are!" However, please do not talk baby talk to your child.

- Vary the tone of voice you use, especially as you narrate your play. You can use different voices for different toy characters.

- For very young children, play games often like *peek-a-boo*, *this little piggy*, and make faces at him. Play "I see you" by smiling at your child and being silly until he responds back.

- Play several times a day for an extended amount of time. Schedule this time **every day**. However, you can take playtime with you and use these techniques when you are away from home. Use it when talking to your child while he is sitting in the shopping cart. Use it while you are waiting for the doctor at his office. Make **every** moment a learning opportunity.

- Playtime is a time when you want to use **as much** language as possible. Playtime is a time to create brain connections so talk, talk, talk. Narrate what your child is doing and narrate what you are doing.

- **Example:** "Ah, I see your truck is carrying blocks around and around the room. It is stopping now. I wonder what the truck is going to do next?"

- Ask lots of questions during the play. Even if your child is not answering, keep on asking.

- What if you cannot get your child to respond to you at all? Then join in whatever he is doing and copy him. If he is jumping around the room, jump around the room. If he is staring at a shadow, stare at the shadow. After doing this for a little bit, start adding variations to what you are doing and see how your child responds.

- Repeat the same play you have done before, but try adding one more thing to it. Then add one more and so on.

- Let your child explore the possibilities. Don't tell him what or what not to do.

- Play imitation games and say, "Your turn!"

- Do not praise your child for responding or connecting to you. Instead, show your enjoyment of the play and how much you are enjoying connecting with your child. You can thank him for playing with you.

- Do not rate your child's play. Do not tell him he played nicely or needs work on anything. This is a non-judgment time.

- Don't let your child stay in his own world for long. Give him many breaks, but come right back to play some more. Take every opportunity to engage with him.

How Is It Done?

Enter your child's play. Sit down at your child's level, greet him, and watch for a little bit. If he is rolling a truck back and forth over and over, put something in front of the truck and say, "Oops! What will the truck do?" Find very small ways to engage in role play during your child's play. Ask many questions. Give him plenty of time to answer you. Ask the questions more than once to show you are waiting for a response. Any response will do including a shrug of the shoulders or making a face at you. Get some sort of response before moving on to the next question or statement. Questions could be, "What is your truck doing? Where is your truck going? Can the truck carry something of mine too?" Even if you are only talking to yourself, narrate everything you are doing. Try different voices. Get creative. Be silly!

Book Nook

Engaging Autism: Using the Floortime Approach to Help Children Relate, Communicate, and Think
Stanley I. Greenspan and Serena Wieder

The Challenging Child: Understanding, Raising and Enjoying the Five "Difficult" Types of Children
by Stanley I. Greenspan and Jacqueline Salmon

www.stanleygreenspan.com/resources/about-floortime

www.icdl.com/dir
(Learn more about the floortime technique)

www.floortime.org
(Learn more about the floortime technique and how to hire a coach)

3

Social Stories

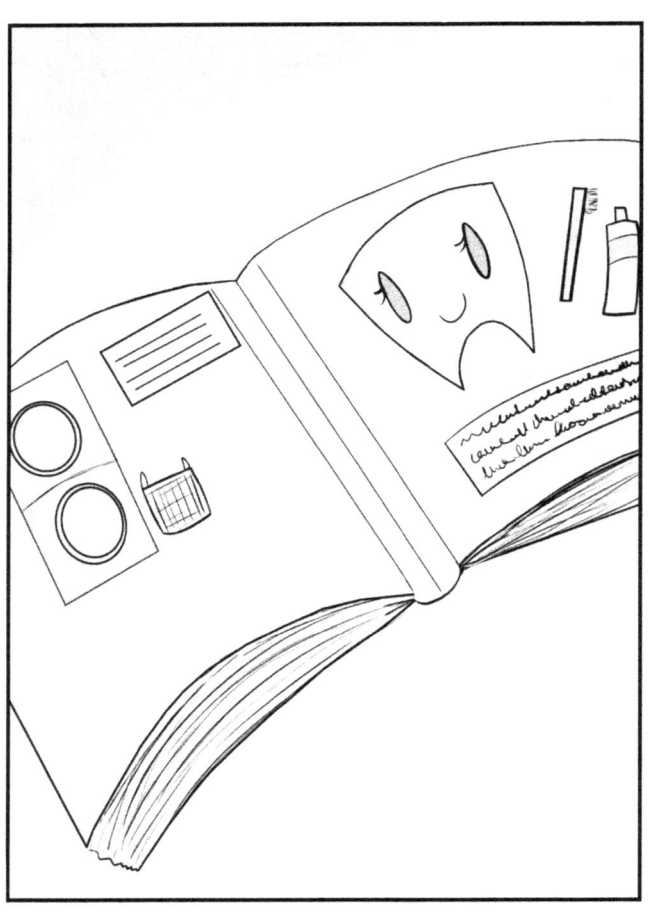

What?

Social stories are a simple way to teach your child the rules of the world around him. You will find them in *The New Social Story Book* by Carol Gray. This is another book I highly recommend buying as you will want to use these stories over and over again. See page 112 for a sample social story.

How?

- ☐ For younger children, read **one** social story to your child every day at the same time. It can be the same story several times in a row.

- ☐ If your child requests a particular story, be sure to include it that day. If he requests the same one over and over, include that story, but add a new one as well.

- ☐ Do not feel the need to discuss the stories with your child. Let the story do the work. Simply by hearing the information within the story, children will *soak up* the rules of social skills.

- ☐ You can stick with one topic for a while or change it daily based on your child's needs.

- ☐ **Do** repeat the same stories. Repetition is vitally important for remembering these rules, especially in stressful situations.

- ☐ Write your own stories based on your child's needs (what he is having difficulty with). Carol Gray teaches you how in her book. The stories are meant to be short and concise so it will not take long to write them. Keep these in a notebook to be reused as needed. For older children use slightly longer stories, but continue to keep them simple.

- ☐ When writing stories, be sure to include your child's interests and things he easily relates to. For instance, if your child loves dinosaurs, include dinosaurs in several of the stories.

- ☐ If your child asks you questions about the story or topic after you read, feel free to answer them and discuss the topic as much as the **child** wishes.

- ☐ Be sure to regularly include stories about the safety issues discussed in First Steps beginning on page 63 and in Next Steps on page 115.

Role-Play!

Even though your child may begin to show that he knows social rules by following them, continue to reinforce by asking questions. "What is the rule about seat belts in the car?" When he answers correctly, compliment him for remembering so well. Also, let your child be the expert for others by asking, "Can you tell Jackson the rule for the most important thing we do before eating?"

What Else?

- ☐ Teach your child about emotions and the body language that accompanies them. How? One way is to use flashcards available on the market from several companies that have a person on each card showing an emotion. Spend regular time teaching this skill. This will be an enormous piece to your child's understanding of the world. If you prefer not to buy the cards, find out if your child's school has a set or will purchase a set for use at school.

- ☐ You can also play, "Name that face" by making faces to show different emotions and see if your child can recognize them.

- ☐ Print an age-appropriate emotions page from the internet, showing cartoon faces of different emotions. Tape it up somewhere around the house or in your child's room so he can practice at any time.

- ☐ While watching a movie or television show with your child, periodically point out emotions shown on the characters' faces. "Oh look, Rusty is sad!"

- ☐ If your child likes to read comic books or Sunday comics, use these as a way to point out interactions between characters. These are an excellent visual way to see how a conversation goes back and forth between people. You can also point out emotions from the drawn faces. Have your child tell you what he thinks the characters are feeling.

☐ Create an emotions chart for your child for each day. Choose several simpler emotions such as happy, sad, mad, etc. You may be able to create this on your computer using emoticons. Just like a chore chart, it may look something like this:

	happy	sad	mad	proud	frustrated	calm
mon						
tues						
wed						
thurs						
fri						
sat						
sun						

Ask your child to fill in or add a sticker to the box that shows how he is feeling each day. If he is not sure at first, tell him to look in the mirror and see which of the faces matches his own.

Important Tip

There are lots of picture books written to teach social rules. Look at the Book Nook in this section for examples of good books to read to your child in order to reinforce the topics you are working on.

Cameron's Corner

"I like social stories if well written. Make sure to personalize them so they will mean more."

Sample Social Story
Written by Emmaline MacBeath

Saying "No Thank You" When I don't Want Something

I am learning to say, "No thank you."

Sometimes people offer me things. They are trying to be nice and generous. Sometimes I want what is offered. Then I say, "Thank you" to be polite. Other times I might not want or like what is being given to me. Then I can say, "No thank you." This means I am happy about the kindness, but I don't want the item.

Here's an Example:

>Once, Grandma offered me broccoli at dinner time. I don't like broccoli so I chose to say, "No thank you." She said, "Okay," and passed the bowl down the table.

>Another time, Uncle George asked me if I wanted some cranberry sauce. I don't like cranberry sauce so I chose to say, "No thank you." Uncle George smiled and said, "You'll like it I promise." Then she put some on my plate. It was okay. My mom says I don't have to eat something I don't want as long as I try one taste. So I said, "No thank you to myself in my head." I tried one taste and then pushed the cranberry sauce to the side of my plate.

My grandma and Uncle George were trying to be nice and helpful to me. Other people try to be nice too.

If I don't like something being offered to me, I will try to say, "No thank you." Then the person will know that I like the helpfulness.

Book Nook

Children's Problem Solving Book Series (picture books)
by Elizabeth Crary
(Offers alternate solutions and outcomes to problems)
   1.   I Want It
   2.   I Can't Wait
   3.   I'm Lost
   4.   My Name is Not Dummy
   5.   Mommy Don't Go

Dealing with Feelings Series (picture books)
by Elizabeth Crary
(Offers ideas for ways to express feelings)
   1.   I'm Frustrated
   2.   I'm Excited
   3.   I'm Mad
   4.   I'm Scared
   5.   I'm Proud
   6.   I'm Furious

Dealing with Disappointment—Helping Kids Cope When Things Don't Go Their Way
by Elizabeth Crary
(teaching emotions)

Please Play Safe! Penguins Guide to Playground Safety (picture book)
by Margery Cuyler

Please Say Please! Penguin's Guide to Manners (picture book)
by Margery Cuyler

That's Good! That's Bad! (picture book)
by Margery Cuyler
(A great way to discuss how a situation can be both good and bad)

When Elephant Goes to a Party (picture book)
by Sonia Levitin
(A delightful story teaching the dos and don'ts of being a guest at a birthday party)

A Learning to Get Along Book (picture books)
by Cheri Meiners
1. Listen and Learn
2. Share and Take Turns
3. When I Feel Afraid
4. Be Polite and Kind
5. Understand and Care
6. Join and Play

Cookies—Bite Sized Life Lessons (picture book)
Amy Krouse Rosenthal
(moral character dictionary)

One of Those Days (picture book)
Amy Krouse Rosenthal
(shows different kinds of days and how they can change into to another kind)

How Do Dinosaurs... (picture book series)
Jane Yolen and Mark Teague

www.carolgraysocialstories.com
(Learn more about social stories and how to use them)

Special Section—Teaching Safety 2

Take every opportunity to teach your child how to keep himself safe. Below are more topics about safety that should be addressed.

Teach The Law

- ☐ Make sure your child understands the law. Tell him which rules you are teaching that are actually laws and punishable by the law if disobeyed.

- ☐ Teach your child how to behave if ever approached by a police officer. Stress that the worst thing he could ever do is to run.

- ☐ Talk about what to do if your child is with someone who is breaking the law.

Bullies

- ☐ Discuss bullies with your child (what is a bully and what they do) and what to do if confronted or bothered by a bully.

- ☐ If your child has had trouble with bullies in the past, include school staff while creating a plan of what to do if your child is approached again.

- ☐ Ask your child to tell you if he is ever bothered by a bully so you can discuss it together and decide what to do.

Book Nook

Bully (picture book)
by Judith Caseley

Just Say No!

- ☐ Again, discuss peer pressure with your child. Talk about reasons why peers may try to pressure him into doing things he doesn't want to do or things he shouldn't do.

- ☐ List as many things as you can think of that peers may ask your child to do that he should say *no* to.

- ☐ Talk about reasons why your child might feel that he should say *yes* and help him think through this problem.

Social Media Safety

Remind your child that social media should be treated no differently than being face to face with someone. Here are some other rules to follow while using social media:

- ☐ Play nice. If you wouldn't say or do something to a person while with them, don't do it online.

- ☐ Keep it appropriate. Once something is posted online it may be there forever. Think before you click.

- ☐ Don't respond to mean messages. Show to them to a parent and then delete.

- ☐ Don't post pictures without permission from a parent.

☐ Add only people you actually know to your friends lists.

Internet Safety

Discuss with your child that not everyone online is who they say they are. They may be lying about who they are to get something from you. Therefore, everyone met online should be treated as a stranger and rules of strangers apply. Here are some more rules of the internet:

☐ Never share personal information of any kind including your last name, address, phone number, age or description as well as personal information of friends or family members.

☐ Never send pictures to strangers.

☐ Don't tell your passwords to anyone except your parents.

☐ Never open emails from strangers as these may contain viruses.

☐ Don't open suspicious emails even if they are from a friend. Have a parent check it out first.

☐ Do not agree to meet with someone who you first met online.

☐ If anything seems weird or strange, ask your parents to check it out.

What Else?

The car is a great time to practice, "What would you do if...?" Come up with different scenarios every car trip. Ask all of your children what choices they would make and then discuss possible consequences of those choices as well as offering more good choices.

4

Introduce New Sensations: Sensory Integration

Why?

Sensations of all kinds are all around us. Your child needs to learn how to cope with these sensations. Sensory integration is a way to build up your child's ability to deal with sensory input slowly over time.

How?

- ☐ Remember to build up slowly over several weeks and months to your child's tolerance level. Do not let your child become too overwhelmed or she will shut down rather than learn.

- ☐ Pick one sensation activity a day. Spend only a couple of minutes on each activity unless your child is truly enjoying herself.

- ☐ Tell your child how you feel about each sensation and then ask how she feels as a comparison. You might touch a feather to your face and say, "I think this feels soft, how does this feel to you?" Exaggerate facial and body expressions so your child can see what soft means to you. Then let her touch it to her own face. Don't force her if she won't touch the feather. Instead, model on yourself again and ask the question again. Try this a few times before stopping. By not forcing your child, you are showing her that you are a safe teacher she can trust. If your child says that she doesn't think the feather is soft ask her how it feels to her. Then ask her what she would think feels soft.

- ☐ Let your child be in control of her feelings about sensations. Do not try to force her to like or feel the same about anything. Simply introduce new sensations.

- ☐ Gradually increase the amount of time in sensory play.

- ☐ Wherever you choose to do sensory integration, provide several things in that room from the sensory list that follows that will stimulate all the different senses.

- ☐ Introduce new foods with different tastes and textures. Don't expect your child to like it or eat it, but do ask her to at least taste it.

- ☐ Continue to keep sensory input calming for the majority of your child's day through the use of low lights, sunglasses, quiet music, and so forth. This will help her to feel calmer and better able to try new things.

- ☐ Check in occasionally to be sure your child's room and comfy spot are still meeting her needs. As she overcomes some sensory issues, her environment may need to change accordingly.

- ☐ To be certain your child is writing with the correct hand, ask your child's eye doctor, occupational therapist or physical therapist to show you how to check which is her dominant hand. Using the correct hand makes a difference in perception.

- ☐ Work with a physical therapist or an occupational therapist to create specific sensory integration activities for your child.

- ☐ Try these sensory rich activities: Bath time play, help in the kitchen, arts and crafts, gardening, and spending a short amount of time (5-10 minutes) in the sunshine with eyes closed (to soak up some sun).

Try the following sensory activities. For safety, choose ones which are age appropriate for your child. Many of these activities help strengthen more than one sensation category.

Touch—Tactile

- Clay
- Play-Doh
- Finger paint (Or paint using food items such as pudding or whip cream.)
- Outdoor chalk
- Make bean bags to toss, from different fabrics that have different textures
- Plastic massage balls with spikes (found in physical therapy catalogs) These can be rolled on the floor or very gently rolled on the body.
- Mystery Items (Blindfolded, your child tries to figure out, through touch, what each item is when placed in front of her.)
- Put together metal nuts, washers, and bolts
- Place beads on a string
- Cut up colorful paper to create confetti
- Stampers and ink
- Use sandpaper on wood
- Water play (squeeze water out of sponges, wash toys, sh)
- Sand play

Taste—Gustatory/Oral

- Blow through a straw into soapy water to make bubbles
- Blow through a straw to move a cotton ball
- Taste test different flavors (include sweet, sour, salty, bitter)
- Blow on a pinwheel
- Blowing bubbles
- Chew gum
- Massage the gums with a fingertip or gum stimulator

Smell—Olfactory

- Aromatherapy

- Mystery Smells (Blindfolded, your child tries to name each smell placed under her nose.)

Sight—Visual
- Kaleidoscope
- Lacing books
- *I Spy* picture books
- *Magic Eye* books
- Put beads on a string

Hearing—Auditory
- Shakers
- Rattles
- Drum
- Play chimes or bells
- Play sounds from different instruments (also try guessing the instrument)
- Play the game *Telephone* (one person whispers a secret and passes it on)
- Listen to different types of music
- Listen to animal sounds and try guessing the animal
- "Tell me what you hear" with eyes closed
- Play *Name that Tune* (pick songs your child would know)

Balance—Vestibular
- Jump on a small indoor trampoline (also called a rebounder)
- Swinging
- Merry-go-round (go gently!)
- Balance board
- Balance beam (or tape a line on the floor)—Walk sideways, forwards and backwards
- Balance ball
- Jump over short objects or off of objects low to the ground

Body In Space—Proprioception
- Massage
- Hammer nails in a thick board or tree stump (Use safety glasses and supervision)
- Provide a mirror to look into
- Roll around on the floor
- *Simon Says* touch the part of your body named

Self-Regulation
- Practice moving fast to slow and slow to fast
- Practice talking softly, then loudly, then softly again
- Touch a hard object, then a soft object
- Play *Green light, yellow light, red light* and go fast, slow and then stop
- Play musical chairs
- Use a metronome and move to the exact beat
- Play music while the child moves. When the music stops, everybody stops.

Role-Play!

Name different items and ask, "How do you think that feels?" or "What does that sound like?" If your child says she does not know, tell her, "I think it feels like…" or "I think it sounds like…" If the item is available, show your child what it is like in reality. Try looking the item up on the internet to see it or hear it. Then ask again, "What do you think it feels like or sounds like?" For instance, "What does a cow sound like?" or "What does a banana feel like?" or "Does mustard taste sweet like sugar?" This will help your child think about the world around her.

Book Nook

Raising a Sensory Smart Child: The Definitive Handbook for Helping Your Child with Sensory Processing Issues
by Lindsey Biel & Nancy Peske

The Out of Sync Child Has Fun
by Carol Stock Kranowitz
(sensory integration activities)

I Spy
by Jean Marzollo & Walter Wick
(book series for visual scanning)

Asperger Syndrome and Sensory Issues—Practical Solutions for Making Sense of the World
by Brenda Smith Myles
(sensory integration—especially helpful ideas for when a child is at school)

Early Intervention Games: Fun Joyful Ways to Develop Social and Motor Skills in Children with Autism Spectrum or Sensory Processing Disorders
by Barbara Sher

Magic Eye Books: A New Way of Looking at the World
by N.E. Thing Enterprises
(learning to see in 3D)

Important Tip

Even though your child is trying new sensations and becoming more comfortable with many of them, there will still be certain sensations that are especially comfortable and certain sensations that are particularly difficult for her. Be aware of this and let her continue to spend more time with the comfortable ones and less time with the difficult ones. We all like our favorite cuddly item and dislike certain things such as the sound of fingernails down a chalkboard or the smell of dirty socks.

Cameron's Corner

"Leave sensory play items out in a designated spot to be played with and your child may become curious and play with them on her own."

Special Section—Attitude Check!

There is no doubt about it—no matter how much we love our children, helping them achieve success is hard work! Let's think about that for a moment.

It is so easy to get sucked into the negative side of things. It is easy to complain about the hard work we have to do. Give yourself some time each week to stop and think about why you are doing the work. Think about the amazing child God has given you and how much the effort is worth to see him make connections, make friends, and enjoy life.

Make a list—mentally or in your family planner—of all the wonderful things about your child. Add to it as you go through the grind of each day. Each time you see a small success, or share a bit of joy, relish it to the fullest.

Remember, your child will pick up on your attitude. If he feels you don't want to do the work, he may not want to either. Model a positive attitude for him. Show him that hard work is part of life if you want the big payoffs.

Be encouraged and full of hope. Be optimistic and use your sense of humor, often. Be patient. Believe that you are making a difference in your child's life. Today you are walking on rocky ground. Soon, the path will become smoother!

5

Slowly Introduce Changes in Routines

Why?

Up to this point, you have been working hard to keep things the same to help your child remain calm and comfortable. But it is not realistic to keep doing this indefinitely. It is time to teach your child that it is safe to be flexible as well as how to deal with change. This is a very difficult skill for the ASD child so go slowly. Begin with one change a week. When this is going smoothly, add one more change and so on.

How?

- ☐ Use Social Stories that deal with change before beginning any changes in routines so your child is already familiar with the topic.

- ☐ Continue to give plenty of advanced warning before any changes in routines happen. Reassure your child that the change will be good and that it is necessary.

- ☐ Whenever possible, give reasons for the changes for better acceptance and understanding.

- ☐ Try recording your child's favorite show and plan an outing during its regular time. Then watch the show when you come back. Don't forget to tell your child ahead of time that this will happen. This will help him see how a change in routine doesn't always mean he has to miss out on his favorite things.

Book Nook

Skill-Building Buddies: For Children with ASD
"Handling Transitions and Change"
DVD 30 min; By Mazzarella Media
(this video is no longer being produced, but you may be able to find a copy on a website like eBay)

☐ During a time when your child doesn't have anything important scheduled (such as a favorite television show) take a short unplanned trip. For example, pick up an item at the grocery store or drop off an item somewhere.

☐ Plan unexpected and unscheduled events your child would enjoy such as inviting a favorite person over to your home, a last minute trip to a favorite park or another place, or an extra amount of time doing a favorite activity—just because. Engage in talk about the positives of the activity.

Role-Play!

Talk about times when schedules may need to be changed and why that may be. Give examples such as emergencies, illness, and helping others. Talk about specific times in your own life when you changed your schedule for one of these reasons. Talk about how you managed a change in your schedule by moving activities to other times or dropping events temporarily.

Important Tip

Don't forget that change can be very difficult. Don't throw your child into an ice cold pool. Instead, start with a comfortable temperature and drop it a few degrees at a time. In other words, make changes slowly enough that your child will barely notice it happening.

Cameron's Corner

"Change did not come easily, but it did come eventually. Be prepared to give plenty of comfort as this helps a lot."

6

Show Your Child What Conversation Looks Like

Using conversation to navigate the world is rather like a foreign language to the ASD child. Therefore, it is our job to teach the language of communication and how to use it to get what she wants.

How?

- ☐ Encourage your child to use her words to get what she wants even if those *words* are gestures. If you know what she wants, try giving her the words such as, "Say, 'Help me please.'"

- ☐ Begin giving multi-step directions. Try two-step directions to begin with, and when success is reached, add more. Examples: "Please bring your plate to the sink and rinse it off." (two steps) "Please bring me the book you want, sit in my lap, and I will read it to you." (three steps)

- ☐ Teach idioms using picture books. Whenever you hear someone use an idiom, teach your child what that person is actually saying.

- ☐ Teach non-verbal forms of communication including facial expressions, body language, and gestures. While watching movies and television, point out when someone uses the non-verbal language you are teaching.

- ☐ Play *let's pretend* and practice conversations as if in a play.

- ☐ When reading books out loud, use different voices for each character. Vary your voice tone and loudness as appropriate. Exaggerate a bit so your child can be aware of what you are doing.

- ☐ Watch television and movies together and comment on conversations.

- ☐ Constantly teach new words.

- ☐ If your child makes a mistake, tell her the correct thing to say and ask her to repeat it.

- ☐ Play *dumb*. Pretend you don't understand something. If your child asks for something, point to the wrong item and ask, "Do you want the bear?" If she says, "No," point to another wrong item and ask, "Do you want the car?" Then say, "Oh, I understand. You want the book!" Make this silly so your child understands it is like a game.

- ☐ Teach your child how to start a conversation with *Hello* and *How are you?* and how to end a conversation with *Goodbye*.

- ☐ Have a Discussion about interrupting when someone is talking. Teach your child that if she feels the need to interrupt, to put her hand on the arm of the person she wants to talk to, and wait to be acknowledged before talking.

- ☐ Talk about the importance of eye contact and how people like to be looked into the eye while talking. Some children think they actually are giving eye contact when they are not. Discuss the possibility of looking at the other person's forehead or nose instead, for now, and see if this helps.

- ☐ Continue to narrate everything.
    - "This is how I…"
    - "I am doing…"
    - "You are playing…"

- Narrate wants and needs.
    - "You are cold because you need a jacket."
    - "You are hungry because it is lunch time."
    - "Your brother is crying because he doesn't feel well."

- Make connections out of everything.
    - "Look at that red balloon like the one from your birthday party."
    - "That cat looks similar to Suzie's."
    - "We have a pool. John does too."
    - "These pants are bigger than your old ones because you are bigger now."

- Ask family and friends to help your child practice by asking her questions and describing things around her.

Book Nook

Picture Books by Fred Gwynne which teach idioms:
A Chocolate Moose for Dinner
A Little Pigeon Toad
The King Who Rained
The Sixteen Hand Horse

Amelia Bedelia book series
by Peggy Parish
(These books are full of idioms and creative language)

Helping Children Improve Their Communication Skills: Therapeutic Activities for Teachers, Parents and Therapists
by Deborah M. Plummer

Scaffolding

Scaffolding is building more on top of what you have. In the context of conversations, this means talking more. Use questions as often as possible that include the words **who**, **what**, **when**, **where**, **why** and **how**.

- ☐ If your child points at something, instead of asking, "What do you want?" Describe the item first. "You are pointing at your favorite sippy cup. Do you want a drink?"

- ☐ If your child asks for juice, ask, "What kind of juice do you want?" or "Where would you like me to pour the juice into—the green cup or the red cup?"

- ☐ If you are reading a picture book and your child points to a picture and says, "Bear," describe it. "Yes, that is a big brown bear. What sound does a bear make?" If you receive no response, then answer, "The bear says, Grrr!" You can also ask, "What does a bear do?"

- ☐ Do not allow a conversation to end with one sentence from each of you. Add more until you have built every interaction into paragraphs.

Important Tip

Simply allowing conversation to flow around your child is not enough anymore. You have to engage her. Questions can help accomplish this. Require your child to tell you specifically what she wants in order to get it. Do not give in to the temptation of thinking or talking for your child.

Cameron's Corner

"I learned a lot about conversation by talking to adults and from watching people talking in movies. Social skills classes helped too. If someone starts a conversation with me it is easier. The best way I have figured out good conversation is from making mistakes and getting feedback from others. Unfortunately, that can very hard on both people sometimes due to awkwardness."

7

Encourage Your Child To Try Something New

Why?

Up to this point, your child has been playing it safe, keeping calm, and working within a very familiar world. But the reality is, there is a huge world out there your child needs to know about and understand in order to increase his success. And, the more you tap into the unfamiliar, the more skills he will build socially while learning flexibility.

How?

- ☐ Begin scheduling short outings to new and interesting places. Tell your child what he will see and do and how long you will be there. Remember to give your child an *out* by letting him know that you will leave early if he gets too tired or he simply needs to.

- ☐ Encourage your child to watch a movie with the family at home that he normally wouldn't. Tell him you want to spend time with the *whole* family. It is okay if he plays quietly by himself in the room during the movie.

- ☐ Go to a new park to play. Make it seem like an adventure to your child. Get excited about the possible new play structures there. If it turns out to be a disappointment, say something like, "Oh well, at least we checked the place out and know what's there so we can tell others." Then end the outing doing something else he likes to do.

- ☐ Cook a new food alongside your regular menu. Tell your child you would love for him to taste test just one bite and tell you what he thinks. Of course, if he likes it he can have more! If it doesn't go well, ask him to help you prepare a new food next time. This will give him ownership in the process and may help open up his willingness to try the new food.

- ☐ Go on a *treasure hunt* drive. Give him a short list of things to look for on the drive, and when they are all found, end the drive at a favorite place or with a yummy treat.

- ☐ Ask your child to look at a map of your city and have him pick a spot for a short picnic. Give him a rule on how far away it can be.

- ☐ Take your child shopping to add or change an item in his bedroom or the household decor.

- ☐ Introduce your child to the concept of letting go of old stuff to make room for new by going to garage sales. Tell him the rules of a garage sale and give him a budget he can spend while there.

- ☐ When you are eating or drinking a different food, offer your child a taste to get his opinion.

- ☐ Drive to a familiar place using a new route. Tell your child ahead of time this is what you are doing.

Role-Play!

Be silly and discuss ways you could change common objects. *Imagine it!*

- "What would it be like if a cat barked instead of meowed?"
- "What would purple apples taste like?"
- "What if we lived in a spaceship?"
- "What would you do if you woke up with a snout in place of your nose?"
- "What if we ate only leaves from trees for food?"
- "What would happen if we ate off the floor instead of at the table?"
- "What would it be like if we drove boats instead of cars?"

> ### Important Tip
>
> Make this a whole family adventure. Trying new things can be fun for everyone. Let each child have a turn picking a new place to go, a new type of food to try, a new DVD to watch, a new CD to listen to, or a new activity. You will be expanding the world for your whole family while cooperating to help your child with ASD become comfortable with new things.

> ### Cameron's Corner
>
> "Only give enough information about new things to peak his interest so you don't scare him off. Describe the new thing as something great! Then be sure to tell him what benefit he will get out of it, because this will matter."

8

Begin To Give Your Child More Complicated Choices

What?

You have been offering your child choices and giving her some of the control. Now it is time to teach her how to narrow down her choices on her own and to learn how every choice has a positive or negative consequence.

How?

- ☐ Begin to allow natural consequences for your child's behavior. If she accidentally makes a mess, she should clean it up. If she makes a mistake, she should fix it. If she upsets someone, she should apologize. Look at the book **Parenting with Love and Logic** for more help on this.

- ☐ If your child does not know how to solve a problem or what choice to make, ask her if she would like for you to offer some choices.

- ☐ Set boundaries by continuing to teach and enforce the rules at home and in the social world.

- ☐ Major on the major issues. Always enforce choices that have to do with safety and health, but be more flexible on minor issues. If your child wants to wear red socks with green pants on July 4th—even if you prefer she wear red, white, and blue—let her. Let her know that you notice her choice. "I notice you **chose** red socks with green pants today." Use a neutral voice with no judgment.

- ☐ Allow your child to be a part of family decision making. Let her choose one or two meals for the weekly menu. Let her write foods she wants to eat on the grocery list. Let her choose the next outing. Let her have a say in which chores will be hers each day.

- When a problem arises, first ask her what she will choose to do about it. Don't offer solutions right away. Let her have time to think about it on her own. If she doesn't come up with choices, then ask, "Do you need help?" When she does offer a choice, ask her how she thinks that choice will work out. If she only shrugs her shoulders for an answer that's okay. Your job is to get her to begin thinking about how choices affect her. Don't think for your child. Always give her extra time to figure things out on her own before stepping in to help.

- Begin to ask some open-ended questions without choices. "What would you like for lunch?" "What movie would you like to watch?" "What park do you want to play at?" If she offers an inappropriate choice like chips and soda for lunch, remind her, "the rule is," and steer her towards a better choice.

- Do require your child to accomplish regular age-appropriate chores every day. Teach her how to do them step by step. Then step back and expect her to complete the tasks on her own. This will help her learn participation and follow through, and will build self-esteem. Praise her for completing the task rather than on how well she completes it.

- Begin raising your expectations a little at a time for your child. Remember to go slowly! Start working on things you have let go of in the past because they were not important at the time. Examples may be incorrect behaviors, how your child responds to you, and compliance.

Role-Play!

Begin teaching your child to think for herself by asking questions like:

- "How do you feel about that?"
- "What do you think about that?"
- "How do you think that will work out?"
- "What do you think will happen?"

If she doesn't reply, don't answer for her. Ask her more specific questions referring to the possibilities like:

- "Do you think she will get mad?"
- "Do you feel angry that she took your book?"
- "Do you think that will help get you what you want?"
- "Do you think the dog will learn to sit by that method?"

Again, don't judge or negate your child's answer by disagreeing. This is your child's chance to have an opinion and to begin discovering how her actions affect things.

Important Tip

Begin having weekly family meetings. A half-hour to an hour is an ideal amount of time. This can be done at the dinner table if pressed for time, but is best done at its own place in the schedule. Talk about the week. Talk about problems that may have come up and brainstorm possible solutions. Talk about your family's schedule for the week and how it will all be accomplished. This is a great time to ask, "How is everything going?" Once this meeting becomes a routine, you will be surprised how your children will open up to you and talk about their week or unsolved problems.

Cameron's Corner

"While more choices meant freedom to me, it was also hard because I didn't always know what to choose. But at the same time, I learned how to make better choices from my mistakes."

9

Give Your Child Tools He Needs For Self-Management

Why?

As much as we as parents want to, we cannot always be there with our children and we can't always be watching closely for cues that a meltdown is on its way. Teaching your child how to calm himself will help both of you and reduce stress when things get difficult.

How?

- ☐ Use Social Stories written for the subjects of frustration, anger, and not getting what is expected.

- ☐ Teach your child the 5-point scale as shown in the book by Karen Dunn Buron and Mitzi Curtis called *The Incredible 5-Point Scale: Assisting Children with Autism Spectrum Disorders in Understanding Social Interactions and Controlling their Emotional Responses.* This is a simple but wonderful concept. Many children with ASD understand numbers better than anything. Using a number scale can help your child understand when he is about to lose control. If this concept works well for you, try the other books about the 5-point scale by these authors.

- ☐ Let home be a safe place for him to de-stress and relax.

- ☐ Create a routine together for times when a tantrum is coming on.

- ☐ Teach positive self-talk. Teach your child to say things to himself like, "I'm okay", "I have choices", "I can get help if I need it", "I'm safe." An important part of teaching this is modeling. When he is upset, say phrases like these to him over and over. He will quickly catch on. ("You are okay," "You are safe," and so on.)

☐ When your child becomes agitated, teach him to distract himself by pointing out things he senses around him. Start modeling this by asking him things like, "Point to something green", "Tell me something you hear", and "Do you smell that baking bread?"

☐ Put a squeeze ball in your child's travel bag. Take it out and give it to him when he is becoming agitated.

☐ Remind him to breathe when he gets upset. Teach him to count to ten slowly to help himself to calm down before he thinks about solutions to his problem.

☐ Teach your child to apologize when he has done something wrong towards someone else even if he didn't purposely do the behavior. Tell him that apologizing shows you care about the other person's feelings and that you want the person to feel better.

☐ When your child is melting down, ask yourself these questions before acting:
        1) What do I need right now?
        2) What does my child need?
        3) Can we both get what we need?
        4) If yes, how?
        5) If no, whose need is most important at this moment?

Role-Play!

Be a good role model. When you are upset, show your child ways in which you calm yourself. Say, "I am very frustrated right now so I am counting to ten before solving this problem." Then close your eyes and breathe deeply. When finished, open your eyes and say, "Okay, I am calmer now and can deal with this." Try this when your child is beginning a tantrum and see what happens.

- "I am too upset to discuss this right now so I am going to my room to calm down. Then we can talk about it."
- "I am too tired to think about this right now. Let me rest for a bit and then we can talk about it."
- "I am very tense. I am going on a walk to relax."

Model to your child what you would like to see him do when he is frustrated or needs something.

Important Tip

Don't forget that when your child melts down or blows up, he usually cannot help it and feels very badly about behaving poorly. Be sure to give him time to calm himself and to get away from the situation before discussing the problem and helping him work through it. Tell him that everyone gets upset at times and remind him of ways to handle things without hurting or upsetting others.

Cameron's Corner

"I have learned to listen to my music or go to my room alone when I am upset. When I am in public and upset, I step off by myself and listen to music on my headphones until I calm down. When the atmosphere at home feels negative, I need to leave and go outside."

Book Nook

The Incredible 5-Point Scale: Assisting Children with Autism Spectrum Disorders in Understanding Social Interactions and Controlling their Emotional Responses
by Karen Dunn Buron and Mitzi Curtis

Children's Problem Solving Book Series (picture books)
by Elizabeth Crary
(Offers alternate solutions and outcomes to problems)
    1.   I Want It
    2.   I Can't Wait
    3.   I'm Lost
    4.   My Name is Not Dummy
    5.   Mommy Don't Go

Dealing with Feelings Series (picture books)
by Elizabeth Crary
(Offers ideas for ways to express feelings)
    1.   I'm Frustrated
    2.   I'm Excited
    3.   I'm Mad
    4.   I'm Scared
    5.   I'm Proud
    6.   I'm Furious

Special Section—Nonverbal Children

Some children with ASD do not speak. There are many different reasons for this. It is important to work with a speech therapist to help you in assisting your child to succeed even while not speaking. In most cases, your child's school will be required to provide speech therapy services for you. Here are a few more things you can try out to help your child navigate the world without using speech.

- ☐ Use hand signals. A good way to come up with these is by using baby sign. This is simplified sign language. (see the following Book Nook.) Encourage your child to signal when she wants something. Encourage her to point to things by saying, "Show me with your finger which cookie you want."

- ☐ If your child is older, consider learning sign language with your child.

- ☐ Try using the computer as a communication device. Some children are unable to verbalize their thoughts, but have no problem typing them on a computer.

- ☐ Consider using PEC or Picture Exchange System. An alternative to sign language, this is a series of picture cards that can be used to communicate. If she wants a glass of water, she hands you or points to the picture of a glass of water. You can purchase these ready made or use your digital camera to take pictures around the house or print clip art and create your own.

- ☐ The DIR®Floortime™ Technique, discussed in the Play Time section beginning on page 100, can help nonverbal children.

Book Nook

Baby Signs
by Linda Acredelo & Susan Goodwyn

When the Brain Can't Hear—Unraveling the Mystery of Auditory Processing Disorder
by Teri James Bellis

A Picture's Worth—PECS and Other Visual Communication Strategies in Autism
by Andy Bondy & Lori Frost

www.autismshopper.com
(for PECS and storybooks)

Special Section—Single Parents

Helping your child succeed may a challenge, but single parents can pull it off too. A very important factor will be to find a way to create a *village* for your family so the burden doesn't fall wholly on you.

How?

- ☐ Don't expect to do everything yourself. Begin with family. Find out who is willing to help and tell them ways they can help you. Some ways might be babysitting, back up during meltdowns, rides to appointments, and helping with at-home therapy or floor time play.

- ☐ Put these helpers on a schedule. People dropping in *whenever* may cause more stress. Also, find out if they would be available to be called on in an emergency during certain times of the day, week, or month as needed.

- ☐ Who else can help? Consider friends, church members, community club members, or college students needing volunteer service hours.

- ☐ Be careful about who spends time alone with your child. Only leave trusted people with him. All others can help you at home while you get other things done such as housework.

- ☐ Don't be afraid to ask for help. This will make the journey easier.

- ☐ Don't worry that you may not have enough time to spend with your child helping him to succeed. Make every moment count by turning everything you do into a learning opportunity.

SCHOOL

At this point, it is hoped that your child is on an IEP and in some kind of rhythm at school. What else should you be doing to ensure her success at school? Here are a few ideas.

- [ ] If you have time, become a volunteer at your child's school a couple of hours a week. This helps your child know you are around if anything really difficult comes up and helps you understand her school environment better. If you choose to volunteer in her classroom, know ahead of time that this may actually make things more difficult for her and be prepared to bow out if this becomes an issue.

- [ ] Check to see if the classroom teacher is teaching to your child's learning style. If she is visual make sure she is getting lots of things to look at in order to learn. If she learns by hearing, she may take tests better if they are given orally. Ask for this option. If she learns by doing, ask for ways she can use her hands such as working on a laptop computer.

- [ ] Make sure your child can ask for small breaks when she needs them.

- [ ] Ask the teacher to create hand signals between herself and your child for times when she needs redirection.

- [ ] Ask for your child to be given extended time on tests and assignments as needed.

- ☐ If your child's IEP did not include social skills education, ask the school to provide a social skills group. There are often other children requiring the same service.

- ☐ Have regular meetings a couple of times a month with the teacher, if possible, to discuss how your child is doing, how you can help encourage progress at home and to brainstorm ways to help her succeed in school. Be sure to include conversations about sensory needs.

- ☐ Find out if there are after school groups your child could attend with supervision or if a club that could be started.

- ☐ Ask your child questions to see if what is listed on the IEP is being provided. If accommodations are not being provided, discuss this with the person in charge of the IEP.

DIET

Again?

It is time to look at your child's diet and reevaluate. Have you removed some foods from the diet such as dairy, gluten or fast food? Have you seen any positive effects? Sometimes positive effects can take a few weeks to show. If you weren't successful before, give it another try.

What Else?

- ☐ Continue to provide whole foods that are not processed. This puts less stress on the body. Whole foods come straight from the earth with vitamins and minerals intact and are much easier to digest.

- ☐ Consider buying only meat and dairy that have not been treated with hormones or antibiotics. Again, this will give the body fewer chemicals to process.

- ☐ Consider adding a probiotic to your child's nutrition. This includes yogurt if dairy is okay. Probiotics can help improve digestion.

- ☐ Consider adding fish oils to your child's diet. Possible choices are cod liver oil or salmon oil. They come in capsules or liquids specifically made for children. These are great sources of Omega-3 oil which has an anti-inflammatory effect on the body.

- ☐ Continue to limit sugar intake. Sugar revs the body up, making it more reactionary, when your goal is to calm it down.

- ☐ Keep caffeine to a minimum as this overstimulates the body. Cut back on or eliminate soft drink consumption. These are full of sugar and zero nutrition. Make sure your child drinks plenty of water instead.

- ☐ Avoid fried foods. They have little to no nutritional value.

- ☐ When cooking vegetables, steam them instead of boiling to keep more nutrients intact.

- ☐ If you are having trouble getting your child to eat vegetables or fruits, puree them and sneak them into other foods like soups.

- ☐ Don't let your child skip meals on a regular basis. Encourage him to at least eat a small snack each time.

- ☐ If your child has digestive issues, be careful of antibiotics which kill good bacteria in the belly. If antibiotics are becoming much too common in your child's life, get a second opinion from a natural health practitioner. If your child must be on antibiotics, give him probiotics at the same time to replenish the good bacteria.

SOCIAL TIME

Now it is time to slowly begin introducing your child to more social situations in order to learn how to navigate them. Remember, social skills have to be taught, as this does not come naturally to your child. Do not push him. Simply let things happen slowly and teach him rules along the way. Expect mistakes and mishaps at this point because he doesn't know and understand all that is expected of him. Don't punish these mistakes, but use them as learning opportunities. Safety in all situations is his primary goal. Remember, until your child feels safe, he will not care about socializing. Take things one small step at a time. Become your child's guide in what feels like a foreign land to him.

How?

- Family time is one of the best and safest feeling ways for social practice. Family meals, family outings, family game night and family vacations are times when you can teach your child social rules.

- Playing family games is an especially wonderful way to learn. Keep the pressure off your child by having low expectations and expecting mistakes. Make this time about being together. Use this opportunity to teach about taking turns, how to lose gracefully, politeness such as "please", "thank you," and "may I" and following rules. Start with simple games with fewer rules and play the same ones often. You can switch out the games as your child becomes comfortable with family game time. Later, take turns with who gets to pick the favorite game each time.

- ☐ Encourage plenty of parallel play. This is where your child is in a room with another child or children and plays by himself but does not interact with others. You may not think he is picking up any social cues this way, but he is. This is a perfect way for him to slowly become comfortable with being around others.

- ☐ Constantly model social behavior for your child and tell your child the rules. Greet a friend at the grocery store and after saying goodbye, tell your child about saying hello and goodbye when seeing a friend. Go to Grandpa's house and talk about sitting quietly while someone else is talking. Every chance you get, in every situation, tell him the rules.

- ☐ Whenever possible, teach social rules before you go somewhere new.

- ☐ Give your child a chance to practice rules you have taught him. For instance, when you are at the check out counter at the clothing store, ask your child, "We need to buy this shirt, but someone is already at the checkout counter. What should we do?" Let him be the knowledgeable one who tells you how things are done.

- ☐ Do you have a pet? Consider letting your child take over its care. This is a great way for him to learn how to interact without having to talk to a person. If you don't have a pet and your child likes animals, consider getting one.

- ☐ When your child is in a social setting with peers, it sometimes helps to define the space so he does not feel that his personal space may be bombarded by others. This can be done by seating all the children in chairs or on carpet squares.

☐ When watching a movie or a television show with your child, point out ways characters correctly interact with each other. Point out social cues you are currently working with your child on such as greetings and goodbyes, how to take turns conversing, manners, or friends vs strangers. If someone in the show does things incorrectly point this out too. "How sad. Charity forgot to say goodbye to her friend before leaving."

☐ Begin teaching your child which topics are not acceptable to discuss in public such as body talk, private family matters, and truths that are better left unsaid (such as commenting on an ugly shirt).

☐ Create hand signals between you and your child for times when you are in public and need to correct his behavior. This will keep the stress down for both of you.

☐ Play what I call, *the Narration Game,* when you are out and about. This is helpful when you are having to wait patiently in line or waiting for something to start and distraction is needed. Find two people who are interacting, out of hearing range, and together try to imagine what they are talking about and how they are feeling based on their body language. The game can turn into silly fun! This can also be done in front of the television with the sound turned off.

☐ If your child is not in a social group at school, consider finding a group in your community where your child can learn social skills in a controlled environment with a teacher. Check with your school or local autism resources to find out if a group is available.

- ☐ When your child is in a group setting, whether at home, a family gathering or at a social event, videotape him. Then later play this back. This will help him get a better idea of how he interacts with those around him, what that looks like, and how others are reacting to him.

- ☐ Teach manners as a part of learning social rules. Here are some example topics: saying *please, thank you, no thank you,* and *excuse me,* asking permission, table manners, body manners such as coughing, sneezing, nose picking and passing gas, interrupting others, asking and replying to "How are you," knocking on closed doors, and using bad words.

Book Nook

Perfect Pigs—An Introduction to Manners (picture book)
by Marc Brown & Stephen Krensky
(covers manners in different social situations)

The Unwritten Rules of Friendship: Simple Strategies to Help Your Child Make Friends
by Natalie M. Elman & Eileen Moore-Kennedy

How Rude! The Teenagers' Guide to Good Manners, Proper Behavior, and Not Grossing People Out
by Alex Packer
(You can use this to help you write social stories on manners and to find specific topics to teach about manners)

EXERCISE

In the Basic Steps section, exercise was primarily a way to calm the body. Now it is time to add some more challenging and stimulating activities. But, don't leave behind activities that calm your child. Continue to add these on a regular basis.

What?

- ☐ Many children with ASD have difficulty with balance. A few times a week, help your child engage in balance activities. These may include bicycle riding, a balance board, rolling and bouncing on a balance ball, a balance beam (use a 2x4 on the floor), jump rope, and playground equipment.

- ☐ Play *Simon Says* exercise style. Give your child different movements to perform. Then let her take a turn and tell you what to do. This would be a perfect game for parallel play with other children.

- ☐ Continue to encourage quiet, deep breathing for a few minutes several times throughout the day.

- ☐ Consider indoor games such as pool, ping pong, or foosball. Find out if there is a community center or activity center in your area that provides these type of games.

- ☐ Create a small obstacle course in your backyard.

- ☐ Play horseshoes, croquet, badminton, bocce, ring toss, frisbee, tether ball, or fly a kite.

- ☐ Play tug of war.

- ☐ Play ball games such as catch, kicking a soccer ball, or shooting baskets with a basketball.

- ☐ Continue using playground equipment. Try different parks with different kinds of big toys.

- ☐ Find a gymnastics center that has open play time or classes.

- ☐ Go bowling, play miniature golf, or roller skate. Keep the time limited to your child's comfort level.

- ☐ Take your child swimming. Water can be very soothing as well as beneficial to balance and muscle tone. It is quieter at pools during lap swim hours. Ask the pool staff if you can come at that time and use a lane for therapeutic swimming.

- ☐ Consider an exercise class where the child learns beside others but doesn't often engage with them, such as karate, yoga or dance.

- ☐ Teach your child playground games like four square and hopscotch.

- ☐ Consider Equine (horse) therapy.

- Learn to juggle together.

- Provide your child with about 30 minutes a day of regular activity and at least half of that outdoors when possible.

Book Nook

101 Games and Activities for Children With Autism, Asperger's and Sensory Processing Disorders
by Tara Delaney
(These activities are labeled by the senses they engage as well as having different levels of difficulty)

Yoga for Children with Autism Spectrum Disorder
by Dion Betts & Stacey Betts

Learn to Move—Move to Learn—Sensorimotor Early Childhood Activity Themes
by Jenny Clark Brack
(Activities that work with all senses and motor skills. Although it is written for early childhood, it would be great for those with ASD)

www.bodymindcentering.com
(Learn more about using mind-body techniques to improve the health of mind and body)

Services That Cost Money
(But May Be Worth Their Weight In Gold)

No one intervention will work for **all** children and **no** one intervention will do everything your child needs. Create an individualized intervention program based on your child's needs, his personality, his likes and dislikes, and his learning style.

How do you know where to begin? Start with any recommendations made based on the testing from when your child was diagnosed with ASD. Talk to your child's teacher, other school personnel involved with your child's IEP, and any professionals you have worked with so far. And finally, talk to other parents of children with ASD. Find out what has helped them make the most progress.

Please note that many mainstream healthcare professionals will not recommend many of the following interventions for a child with ASD. They may cite that scientific evidence does not support their use. This does not mean these interventions have not helped create success for many children. Investigate each intervention thoroughly and what it is expected to do for your child before considering its use. Also, for the best results. find the highest quality provider available.

THERAPIES

Physical Therapy

- **What it is:** Work done by a health professional to treat issues relating to physical function. This may include education, exercises, or adaptive devices.
- **How it helps:** It helps children having problems with balance, coordination, strength, motor skills, pain with movement, neurological issues and sensory integration.
- **Positives:** Physical therapists are highly trained. They can give specific exercises to alleviate problems. It is research based.
- **Negatives:** It can be very costly if not provided through school or health insurance. You may have to travel to a clinic. It may require a lot of work at home.
- **Amount of Sessions:** Varies with need

Occupational Therapy

- **What it is:** Work done by a health professional to treat issues relating to functional independence (daily living skills).
- **How it helps:** It helps children having problems with sensory integration, motor skills, developmental activities, self-regulation, self-care, and social skills.
- **Positives:** Occupational Therapists are highly trained. They work with specific tasks and exercises to alleviate problems. It is research based.
- **Negatives:** It can be very costly if not provided through school or health insurance. You may have to travel to a clinic. It may require a lot of work at home.
- **Amount of Sessions:** Varies with need

Vision Therapy
- **What it is:** Exercises or special lenses given by a trained vision therapist.
- **How it helps:** It improves visual skills and ability, visual comfort, ease, and efficiency, and processing of visual information. It can improve sensory integration, balance and motor control, as well as many tasks such as reading and writing.
- **Positives:** You may see great improvement very quickly.
- **Negatives:** It can be very expensive. You must spend a specific amount of time daily at home working on exercises. You will need to have your child evaluated by a developmental optometrist to find out what his visual needs are.
- **Amount of Sessions:** Varies depending on need and goals

Auditory Integration
- **What it is:** Listening to filtered and modulated music. It is modified individually for each child.
- **How it helps:** It addresses sensory problems such as hearing distortions and over-sensitive hearing.
- **Positives:** It may reduce discomfort for those with auditory integration issues.
- **Negatives:** Regulated training is not required for this therapy. Although many practicing auditory integration therapists are health professionals, many are not.
- **Amount of Sessions:** The standard is 20 half hour sessions over 10 days

Sensory Integration
- **What it is:** Activities, exercises, and accommodations targeted towards sensory processing issues. It is usually performed by physical or occupational therapists.

- **How it helps:** It treats sensory integration and processing issues. It seeks to balance sensory input and can reduce stimming.
- **Positives:** It can be individualized for each child. It is non-invasive although it may be uncomfortable at times.
- **Negatives:** It can be costly if not provided through school or health insurance. You will probably have to travel to a clinic. Work at home may be involved.
- **Amount of Sessions:** Varies based on need

Neurofeedback

- **What it is:** A type of biofeedback that uses real-time EEG to show the brain its own activity and uses feedback to teach the brain self-regulation. The child has sensors attached to the scalp to read the EEG. Feedback provided may be through sound, light, and vibration.
- **How it helps:** This therapy helps the brain teach itself through feedback which supports positive brain activity and development.
- **Positives:** It is easy to do. The child sits in a comfortable chair in front of a television screen and watches a *game*. The child can sit in a parent's lap during therapy. It can provide relaxation. You may see some results quickly. Sensors can be moved to work on different parts of the brain according to the child's need.
- **Negatives:** Neurofeedback technicians are not necessarily healthcare providers. No training is required or regulated although certification is available. Look for a certified professional. It can be inappropriate for children with certain health conditions such as seizures. If you are unsure, check with your healthcare provider before beginning this therapy.
- **Amount of Sessions:** Varies based on need and agreed upon therapy plan. Look for a provider who is child-friendly and is familiar with working with children with ASD.

Speech Therapy
- **What it is:** Work done by a health professional to help people with speech and language problems.
- **How it helps:** It helps children with articulation, fluency, resonance and understanding, as well as processing and expressing language. Therapy can include adaptive devices.
- **Positives:** Speech Therapists are highly trained. They can individualize a program based on child's needs. It is research based.
- **Negatives:** Although this is a therapy commonly provided by schools, if it is not, it can be expensive.
- **Amount of Sessions:** Varies based on need

Music Therapy
- **What it is:** Uses music interventions to accomplish individualized goals. This therapy is provided by a trained music therapist. Interventions may include singing, listening to, creating or moving to music.
- **How it helps:** Music provides an alternate way of communicating. It can improve physical strength and ease of movement (depending on the type of therapy) as well as a sense of comfort and support.
- **Positives:** It is a non-invasive technique that can be calming. It is easy to engage in. It is usually provided by trained professionals and is research based.
- **Negatives:** It can be expensive.
- **Amount of Sessions:** Varies based on need and number desired

Aquatic Therapy

- **What it is:** Physical therapy performed in the water. Uses the resistance of the water while providing less strain on the joints.
- **How it helps:** It can help with sensory integration, range of motion, as well as strength and balance.
- **Positives:** Provides a supportive environment for physical therapy. It can provide relaxation during therapy. It may be considered more fun by children who like water.
- **Negatives:** It may be provided by many different types of professionals. Be sure to research the provider. It can be expensive. You will need to have access to a pool. Be careful of highly chlorinated pools as this can be a problem for your child. As an alternative, look for a therapeutic saltwater pool in your area.
- **Amount of Sessions:** Varies based on need

Animal Assisted Therapy

- **What it is:** Work with an animal with specific characteristics to meet goals. These animals are incorporated into work already being done such as physical or occupational therapy.
- **How it helps:** It provides a chance for an additional and safe feeling interaction during therapy.
- **Positives:** For children who like animals this can be very motivational.
- **Negatives:** It may not be effective for children who do not like animals. It may be difficult to find someone to provide these services.
- **Amount of Sessions:** Varies based on need

Integrated Movement Therapy

- **What it is:** A combination of Yoga and mind-body techniques. "Each IMT®

session is based on six core principles: structure and continuity, physical stimulation, language stimulation, social interaction, self-calming and direct self-esteem building." (this description is from the website www.bodymindcentering.com)
- **How it helps:** It can help children with balance, ease of movement, coordination, sensory integration, self-regulation, and communication.
- **Positives:** This is a calming therapy.
- **Negatives:** It may be difficult to find someone in your area to provide services, however, there may be similar services in your area if this one is unavailable. Can be expensive.
- **Amount of Sessions:** Varies based on need and desire.

Light Therapy
- **What it is:** Exposure to daylight or a specific type or color of light for a specified amount of time.
- **How it helps:** It is thought to promote healing, reduce inflammation, and provide cell stability.
- **Positives:** Using sunlight for light therapy is free. Light therapy has been proven as helpful under certain circumstances, but its use for ASD is uncertain. Research this therapy further based on your child's specific needs.
- **Negatives:** Light therapy can be dangerous. Those who experience seizures should never undergo light therapy unless it is under the direction of their healthcare professional. It can be expensive depending on the type of therapy. Look for a therapist who is highly trained in his profession.
- **Amount of Sessions:** Varies based on the type of light therapy and need

BIOMEDICAL APPROACHES
(see Biomedical Interventions in the Challenge section on page 185)

BEHAVIORAL APPROACHES

- **DIR®Floortime™ Technique**
  (Discussed in Next Steps: *Play Time*, p. 100)
- **Social Skills Classes**
  (a class that teaches how to interact and communicate with others)
- **Applied Behavior Analysis (ABA) or Discrete Trial Teaching (DTT)**
  (Commonly used, but does not consider emotional and intrapersonal development. Does not teach child higher thinking skills although it can be useful for teaching the specific steps of certain skills.)
- **Individual Counseling**

BODYWORK

Craniosacral Therapy

- **What it is:** This is a therapy intended to relieve pain and tension by gentle manipulations of the skull regarded as regulating the flow of cerebrospinal fluid with a natural rhythm in the central nervous system. It is usually provided by trained massage therapists, chiropractors, or osteopaths.
- **How it helps:** It is thought to relieve headaches and tightness throughout the body, improve sensory processing issues and coordination, as well as helping to calm the nervous system. It may also help with communication and immune system function.
- **Positives:** It does not require long-term use, is non-invasive, and provided in a massage therapy type of environment.
- **Negatives:** Providers can vary widely in quality and technique. Research therapists thoroughly. It may be difficult to find in your area. Do not use on toddlers as it may interfere with skull development or cause injury.
- **Amount of Sessions:** Varies, although usually only a few are required

Acupuncture
- **What it is:** The use of specialized needles along the meridians of the body to promote healing.
- **How it helps:** It can help alleviate pain, improve sensory integration, and calm the nervous system.
- **Positives:** It can be inexpensive depending on the provider, but may be difficult to find a provider in your area.
- **Negatives:** If your child is sensitive to touch this may not be a helpful therapy. Find a licensed provider who only uses sanitized needles.
- **Amount of Sessions:** Varies based on desired outcome and effectiveness

Reflexology
- **What it is:** Massage that uses reflex points in the hands, feet, or ears that are linked to the rest of the body, to alleviate symptoms. Usually performed by a trained massage therapist.
- **How it helps:** It can help alleviate tension and pain, improve immune function and sensory processing, and calm the nervous system.
- **Positives:** For a child uncomfortable with touch this can be a very effective treatment as only a small area on the body is touched. It can be very relaxing.
- **Negatives:** It may be difficult to find a provider in your area and can be expensive.
- **Amount of Sessions:** Varies based on desire and effectiveness.

Bowen Technique
- **What it is:** A hands-on therapy consisting of a specific sequence of gentle, rolling type of moves done across superficial muscles, tendons and nerves that effectively realign the body. It stimulates the tissues and muscles of the

body. It is usually performed by a trained physical therapist, chiropractic practitioner or osteopath.
- **How it helps:** It can correct musculoskeletal problems, help with pain and stiffness, and help with balance, coordination, and ease of movement. It may also calm the nervous system, help improve digestive problems, and help the body in the detoxification process.
- **Positives:** The child lays comfortably on a table which can be soothing. You may see results very quickly.
- **Negatives:** It may be difficult to find a provider in your area. It may be expensive. The child might feel ill or stiff for a few days after treatment before feeling the improvement. This is a hands-on therapy so it could be difficult for children sensitive to touch.
- **Amount of Sessions:** Varies depending on need

There are many more types of bodywork available. Check with your local licensed massage therapist for more information.

INTERVENTIONS THAT MIGHT BE PROVIDED TO YOU FOR FREE

In Your Community:
- Local birth-3 programs

At Your School:
- Speech Therapy
- Occupational Therapy
- Social Skills Classes
- Behavioral Approaches

Book Nook

Seeing Through New Eyes
Changing the lives of children with autism, Asperger Syndrome and other developmental disabilities through Vision Therapy
by Melvin Kaplan

The Out of Sync Child Has Fun
by Carol Stock Kranowitz
(Sensory integration activities)

The Healing Power of Neurofeedback: The Revolutionary LENS technique for Restoring Optimal Brain Function
by Stephen Larsen

Cutting Edge Therapies for Autism
by Ken Siri & Tony Lyons
(This book lists and explains dozens of available therapies)

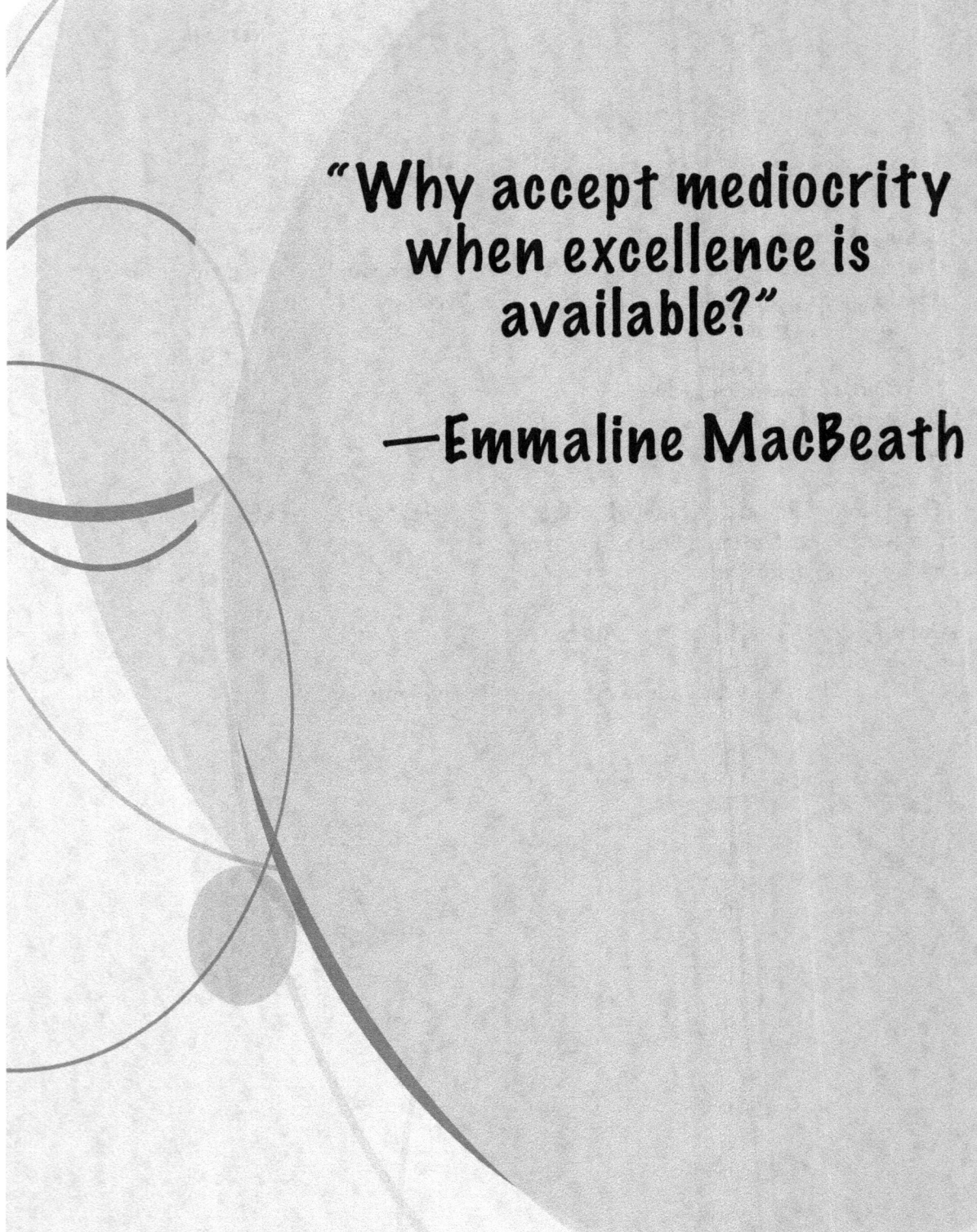

"Why accept mediocrity when excellence is available?"

—Emmaline MacBeath

CHALLENGE STEPS

This section is about building independence. You have been teaching your child, making connections, and inching him out of his comfort zone. Now it is time to expect your child to do more on his own. Lead the way, show him what needs to be done, build his confidence, and then step back and let him do it by himself. Don't despair over mistakes. Use them as opportunities to build upon what you have already taught your child.

Use each of the Positive Self Talk statements, in this section, to teach your child how to build his own confidence. Model them by telling him, "You can learn it." He will soon turn this into, "I can learn it." Now it is time to watch your child grow!

1

Teach Your Child How To Help Himself Overcome ASD (Self-Esteem)

You will not always be around to help your child get through difficult situations. Empowering him to teach himself new skills and to get himself out of tight spots will enable him to navigate the world better and better each day.

How?

- Another book I highly recommend you buy is, *The Survival Guide for Kids with Autism Spectrum Disorder (and their parents)* by Elizabeth Verdick and Elizabeth Reeve. It is full of helpful tips given in a pleasing layout. This book talks to the child rather than the parent. Consider working through it with your child. Talking to your child about each section will show him he still has some help and doesn't have to figure it all out on his own.

- Keep the lines of communication open between you and your child. Let him know he can talk to you about anything and then follow through by simply listening when he has an issue. Even if the issue isn't solved right away, talking it out can be a great relief to him.

- Encourage your child to make a list or to come to you with words, phrases, and situations he doesn't understand.

- Continue to encourage him to do as many things as possible for himself and to use his problem-solving skills.

- Offer compliments on his hard work even when he doesn't meet all of your expectations. Encourage effort rather than judging the work so he will keep trying and will feel good about himself.

☐ Don't forget that children with ASD often have trouble transferring knowledge from one situation to another. Continue to teach, teach, and teach again.

☐ Encourage your child to engage in volunteer work as a way to be out in the social world more. Begin by volunteering beside him, and as he becomes old enough, allow him to volunteer on his own.

☐ Talk about ways for him to explain ASD to others. Discuss who should know and who should not. Explain possible consequences of people knowing or not knowing.

Cameron's Corner

"At this point, I was able to help myself because of everything I had learned and the tools I was given."

Challenge Steps   185

Positive Self-Talk

"I am important"
"I belong"
"I am good enough"
"People believe in me"
"I can learn what I need to know"
"My family and friends love me as I am"
"I am needed"

Book Nook

The Survival Guide for Kids with Autism Spectrum Disorders
by Elizabeth Verdick & Elizabeth Reeve
(Answers questions & provides strategies for kids to learn and to help themselves)

Life Lists for Teens: Tips, Steps, Hints, and How-Tos for Growing Up, Getting Along, Learning, and Having Fun
by Pamela Espeland

The Whole Brained Child
by Daniel Siegel

Six Steps to An Emotionally Intelligent Teenager: Teaching Social Skills to Your Teen
by James Windell

Different, Not Less
Inspiring stories of achievement and successful employment from adults with Autism, Asperger's and ADHD
by Temple Grandin

Emotional Impact Series (picture books)
by Adolph Moser & Dav Pilkey or David Melton
  1) Don't Pop Your Cork on Monday (stress) Pilkey
  2) Don't Feed the Monster on Tuesday (self-esteem) Melton
  3) Don't Rant on Wednesday (anger) Melton
  4) Don't Despair on Thursday (grief) Melton
  5) Don't Tell a Whopper on Friday (truth) Melton
  6) Don't Fall Apart on Saturday (divorce) Melton
  7) Don't be a Menace on a Sunday (violence) Melton

Special Section—Biomedical Interventions

Is Autism Spectrum Disorder a brain disorder or a disorder that affects the brain? This is what experts are currently studying. No matter which way you look at it, there are some similarities in the body that are becoming apparent among the ASD population. These may include digestive issues, food allergies or sensitivities, toxic levels of metals in the system, vitamin deficiencies, high levels of Candida Albicans (yeast), as well as various chemical imbalances.

This is where biomedical treatments can be helpful. These interventions address the needs of the body through medical or chemical means. Again, not all children need all of these treatments. Not all treatments will help all children. Testing is especially important to discover your child's exact needs in order to provide an individualized treatment plan. If your conventional medical doctor will not discuss these choices with you, or provide testing, find a naturopathic doctor who will.

This list is not meant to diagnose or treat anyone. Symptoms vary widely with each individual. Use this list as a guide to ask your doctor questions regarding your child's health.

Begin with Food Allergy Testing

Understand that food allergies and food sensitivities are not the same thing. A child can be lactose intolerant, but not allergic to milk. If the food allergy tests come back positive, completely eliminate that food. It does no good to cut down on the food. If after eliminating these foods for several months you are still noticing food sensitivities, consider testing for food intolerances.

> A Few of the Possible Symptoms of Food Allergies: Rashes, dark circles under the eyes, constipation or diarrhea, partially undigested food in stool, asthma, stomach aches, nausea, acne, itching, runny nose, blood in the stool, poor growth, irritability, or difficulty sleeping

Consider Testing for Candida Albicans (yeast)

Many parents with children on the spectrum have found that their children have yeast overgrowth (often due to repeated use of antibiotics) and were much improved after being treated. Again, you may have to talk to a natural health care provider to accomplish this. Work with a professional and have the testing done before treating.

> Possible Symptoms: The symptom list is vast, but more common ones are rashes especially in moist areas (underarms and groin), cravings for dairy or sugar, irritability, frequent infections that have been treated by antibiotics, digestive issues, foul-smelling stool, headaches, feeling bloated after eating, or rectal itching

Vitamin and Mineral Testing

Quite a bit of literature is available regarding the use of particular vitamins or minerals in larger amounts to help those with ASD. This is tricky, because it is not obvious which children need certain vitamins and minerals just by looking at them or their symptoms. I recommend not giving more than a regular multivitamin without first testing your child's needs. There are tests that can show the levels of vitamins and minerals in the blood. Get a complete test that covers all of the common vitamins and minerals. You most likely will need to see a naturopathic doctor for this kind test. They can be costly, but worth it for the knowledge they provide, especially if a deficiency is found. Do not give large doses of vitamins or minerals to your child unless under the care of a medical or naturopathic doctor. Reaching toxic levels is easy to do with some supplements and can make your child extremely ill.

> Possible Symptoms: Varies with each type of deficiency

Digestive Enzymes

Talk to your doctor or naturopathic doctor about digestive enzymes if your child is still having digestive issues even after a change in diet. Enzymes help your child's body to break down and digest food better. As he is healing it may be a good option. Understand that this is a temporary solution. You do not want your child on these long term as it may eventually interfere with your child's ability to produce his own digestive enzymes. You can also consider a stool test to check for digestive enzyme health. Talk to your child's doctor or natural healthcare provider about the length of time he should take digestive enzymes.

> Possible Symptoms: Continued digestive upset after removing allergic foods, partially digested food in stool, nausea, flatulence, foul-smelling stools, bloating, or feeling full quickly when eating

Amino Acids

Amino acids are the chemical building blocks for protein in your body. Again, like vitamins and minerals, it is difficult to know which amino acids a child may need without proper testing. Before giving these supplements, it is best to have your child's levels tested and have an individualized supplement created for your child. This will give the best result.

> Possible Symptoms: Varies with each type of deficiency

Chelation Therapy

Many children with ASD have been found to have toxic levels of metals in their bodies. It is thought by some that this is due to their bodies' inability to detox the metals from their systems. This could be why the mercury in vaccines prior to 1999 was affecting some children, but not all. Regardless of the reason, it may be worthwhile to test your child for metal toxicity. Testing can be done with hair, blood, or urine. Some doctors do not find the hair test to be a valid indicator. The urine test is done by getting a pre-sample and then a post-sample after giving the child a drug called DMSA or DMPS which pulls metals from tissues and organs. Regardless of the testing method, do not consider chelation therapy of any kind without prior testing.

Chelation is a method of pulling metals from the body. It can be done through IV with a drug called EDTA or through DMSA or DMPS pills. There are side effects of chelation that can be dangerous. Some metal toxicities do not require chelation for removal. Do not attempt chelation therapy without a doctor overseeing the process. The amount of therapy depends on the levels of metals and the effectiveness of treatment.

> Possible Symptoms: Varies with the type of metal toxicity

There are other forms of biomedical interventions available for children to help with various symptoms. Always check with your doctor or natural health care provider before attempting them.

Book Nook

Healing the New Childhood Epidemics: Autism, ADHD, Asthma, and Allergies
by Kenneth Bock
(diet, nutrition, and medical interventions)

Healing our Autistic Children—A Medical Plan for Restoring Your Child's Health
by Julie Buckley
(very clinical but talks about nutrition, supplements, tests)

Enzymes for Autism and Other Neurological Conditions
by Karen DeFelice

Healing and Preventing Autism
by Jenny McCarthy
(A guide for parents to spot early warning signs of Autism, as well as diffusing environmental, chemical and food triggers)

Victory over ADHD—How a mother's journey to natural medicine reversed her children's severe emotional, mental and behavioral problems
by Deborah Merlin and Larry Cook

The Age of Autism—Mercury Medicine and A Man-Made Epidemic
Dan Olmsted & Mark Blaxill

The Autism Enigma DVD
(looks at the possible link between gastrointestinal health and Autism)

2

Teach Your Child To Face And Solve Problems (Problem-Solving)

Why?

Although there will still be times your child needs to leave a stressful situation for a little while, this option won't always be available. Now she needs to learn how to deal with the tough stuff in a comfortable way.

How?

- ☐ When your child gets through a tough spot without losing it, praise her for a job well done! After she has time to calm down and get away from the situation, talk about what else she could do in the future if that problem comes up again.

- ☐ When watching television and movies, point out positive methods the characters use to face problems. On the flip side, point out negative methods they use that don't work out so well.

- ☐ Stress to your child to ask for help when she doesn't know how to handle a difficult situation. Teach her phrases she can use to ask for help like, "I don't know what to do" or "What is the rule here?" I always tell children that asking for help is a sign of how smart they are.

Role-Play!

As often as possible, talk about different scenarios of stressful situations and what can be done to get through them. Discuss more than one choice for each situation, but also keep it simple.

- ☐ Create small problems on purpose and help your child to solve them. An example is to move something from its usual place. See what she does and encourage her to ask you for help only if she needs it. Don't do this more than her tolerance level will allow.

- ☐ Make sure your child knows that mistakes are okay and something to be learned from. Failure is an opportunity to grow.

- ☐ Teach your child the following steps to think through a problem:
    1) Everyone has problems.
    2) Every problem can be solved in some way.
    3) Ask yourself, "What is the problem?" Write it down.
    4) What are the facts of the problem? Write them down.
    5) Tell yourself, "I can solve this problem" and " I will ask for help if I need it."
    6) List possible solutions to the problem.
    7) Ask yourself, "How might each solution work out if I use it?"
    8) Make a plan and put it into action.
    9) If the solution didn't work, try another solution or ask for help.

- ☐ Consider creating a problem-solving journal for your child. Write or glue the above steps inside the front cover.

Book Nook

Do One Thing Different—Ten Simple Ways to Change Your Life
by Bill O'Hanlon

Positive Self-Talk

"I can do it"
"I am good enough"
"I am responsible"
"I can solve this problem"
"I am confident"
"I am a good thinker"
"I trust myself"
"I do what's best for me"

Cameron's Corner

"Problem-solving is easier if you have someone to talk it through with. Other people encourage me to do what needs to be done. Sometimes, when no one is available, I use the internet to find answers."

3

Teach Your Child That Sometimes Rules Change (Flexibility)

Why?

To this point, you have been trying to keep things stable and calm through routine and sameness. But life is constantly changing. Your child needs to learn flexibility.

How?

- ☐ When routines need to change, continue to give your child warnings ahead of time when possible, but be sure to give the reason behind the change. This helps the child make sense of the change more easily.

- ☐ Use Social Stories that talk about change and unexpected things.

- ☐ Think of some things around the house you would like to see improve. One at a time, change a rule to create this improvement. For example: The old rule was to stack your dirty dishes in the sink, but food was getting stuck on the dishes. You can tell your child, "Today we have a new rule in the house. The old rule is…The new rule is to rinse your dish before placing it in the

Role-Play!

Talk about situations when a rule might change. For example: "In the library, books are always returned in the drop box by the librarian's desk. What if the library changes that rule and has the books returned in a slot by the door? Why might the library have had a good reason for this change?"

sink so food doesn't dry on it." Keep rule changes to a minimum so your child can get used to the new rule before time to learn another one.

☐ When going to a new place, ask your child, "What do you think we are supposed to do here? How can you tell?" Teach your child how to look for visual cues to know what the rules are in any place.

☐ Give your child a chance to act out the rules on his own. When buying something, give him the money to complete the transaction while you stand next to him. Praise him simply for completing the transaction no matter whether any mistakes were made. Ask him to run into the library for you to drop off books by himself or give him something that needs to be mailed. Don't give any instructions unless he asks or looks unable to proceed, but do stand by to watch.

Cameron's Corner

"It helps me to know that things are not permanent and everything can change. Expecting change makes it easier when it happens. Although, this is still very difficult for me."

Positive Self-Talk

"I can handle change"
"I am flexible"
"I can like this"
"I am calm"
"New things are good for me"

4

Teach Your Child How To Be Comfortable In The World Of Sensations
(Space Management)

Why?

Your child will not always be in the same place. She needs to learn to manage the environment wherever she is. And when she is in her own space, she needs to know how to make it comfortable for herself.

How?

- ☐ Continue to update your child's trip backpack with items that make her more comfortable, such as snacks, water, headphones, sunglasses, a jacket, a book to read, handheld video games, a music player, and a cell phone. You can even download nature sounds and white noise onto handheld music players.

- ☐ Help your child to learn a better alternative to stimming behavior in order to calm her system such as deep breathing, squeezing a stress ball, using items in her travel pack and asking for help. ("Please close the blinds.", "Can you turn down the music?")

- ☐ Teach your child how to calm herself when she gets home after being gone for the day. Give her 15-30 minutes to do a preferred activity such as quiet time in her comfy spot, time with her hobbies, reading, backyard play, or exercise. Do not expect her to do anything else until she has had time to decompress and relax.

- ☐ If your child is doing well with touch, consider regular massage sessions, or if she is younger, doing the massage yourself. You could try massaging only her hands or feet.

- ☐ Try aromatherapy. Let your child pick out an essential oil that is pleasing to her and put it in a diffuser in her room or a room in the house.

☐ Teach your child how to express how she feels internally. Model this by telling her how you think she feels, "It looks like you are angry," or "I know you are frustrated about having too much homework."

Role-Play!

Talk about what to do if she is out and about and starts to get overwhelmed. Some choices may be: Close your eyes and count to ten, take a trip to the bathroom, leave if it becomes too much, or focus on something pleasant in the room.

In Her Bedroom:
A Clean And Organized Room Is A Happy Room

☐ Create a workspace with good lighting where she can do her homework.

☐ Spring clean with your child every few months. Or if she prefers for you not to touch her things, tell her what is expected and have her clean her room by herself. Encourage her to donate items she no longer uses or wants.

☐ If needed, keep a trash can in her room and expect her to empty it weekly.

☐ Use bins, drawer carts, or baskets to help your child organize her things. If she is visually inclined, put labels on all of the organizers.

☐ Teach your child to clean up her room every night before she goes to bed. This means putting everything away where it goes and throwing trash in the trash can.

☐ On the computer, teach your child how to create and organize files of her things.

☐ Show your child how to clean out her backpack each day by emptying it, sorting, and putting back only what needs to be there for the next day. This is a perfect time to find notes to parents, homework, and trash for the bin.

☐ Help your child organize her school papers. There are many systems including using a binder, two pocket folders, tab dividers, file folders, or a combination of these.

☐ Encourage the one in one out rule. If your child receives or buys something new, ask her to donate an older toy so the amount of her stuff does not outgrow her bedroom.

Cameron's Corner

"When I get stressed in a public space, I've learned to move around. This keeps me from being too stressed. When I can't walk about, I try to focus on positive things or the details around me to distract myself. At home, I go into my bedroom with my door closed to be alone, but I still keep busy."

Positive Self-Talk

"I like myself the way I am"
"I can relax"
"My body is my own"
"I am calm"
"I can handle this"
"I feel comfortable in my space"

Book Nook

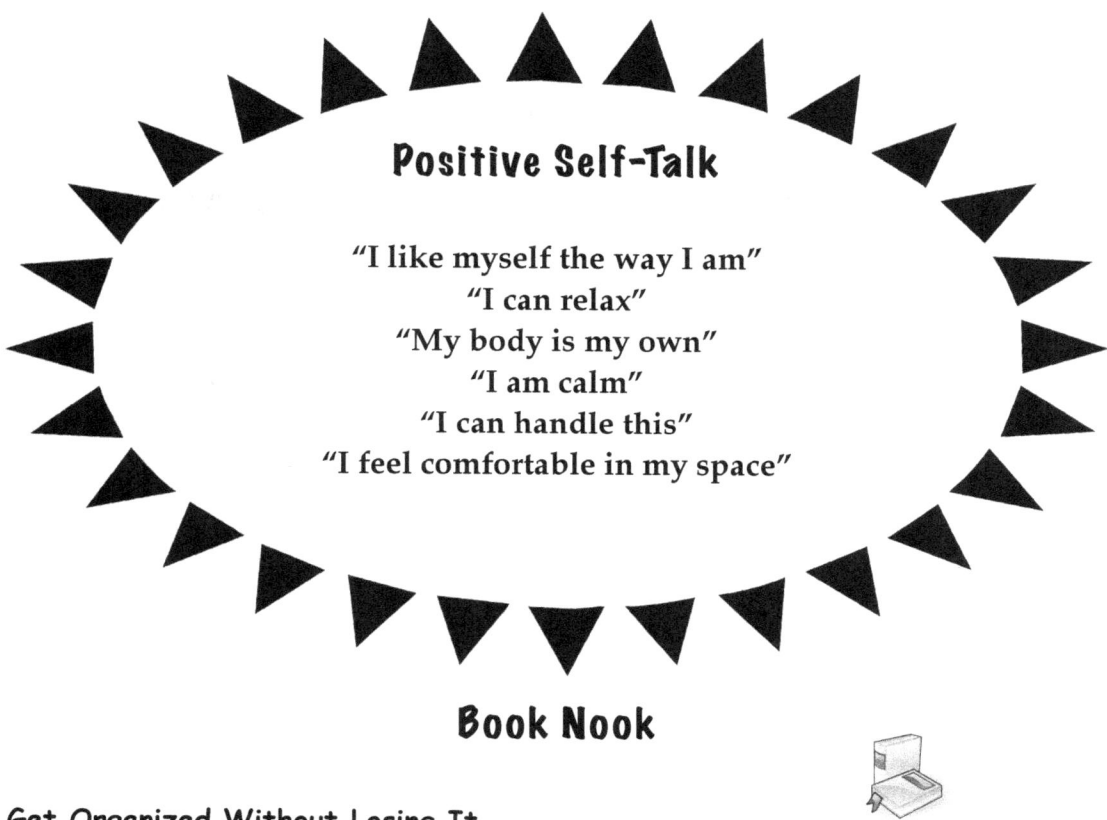

Get Organized Without Losing It
by Janet Fox
(A guide for teens to organize themselves)

The Organized Student
by Donna Goldberg
(A Step by step guide to organizing your student. Good for those who don't know where to start)

Conquering Chronic Disorganization
by Judith Kolberg
(New ways of looking at organizing)

Where's My Stuff? The Ultimate Teen Organizing Guide
by Samantha Moss

5

Teach Your Child To Create His Own Routine And To Adjust
(Time Management)

If your child can learn to manage his own time, he will be more in control of his days and better able to make adjustments as needed.

How?

- ☐ Teach your child how to make to-do lists and then to prioritize. Put the most important items that **must** be done first at the top of the list.

- ☐ Buy a simple organizer or calendar where your child can write down all of the future events in his life. He should not only put events on the calendar, but important deadlines such as tests and project due dates as well. Have him put his items on the family calendar once a week. Show him how to look ahead to what events are happening soon so he can plan his time.

- ☐ Remind your child to put *me-time* into his daily schedule. This is the 15-30 minutes he will need daily for relaxation.

- ☐ Encourage your child not to wait to start on something. Show him how he can do a little bit at a time to get things done. This is especially helpful for the difficult things.

- ☐ Show your child how to break larger tasks down into several smaller ones. For instance, if he has a report on alligators due in one week, show him the steps to complete it which include research and note taking, several sections of writing, finding pictures, and typing the final draft. The report does not have to be done all in one sitting.

- ☐ Use Post-it notes or flashcards as a visual reminder of things your child needs to do. Put Post-its in his room, the bathroom, or the kitchen. You can even use different colors for different types of reminders. Flashcards can travel with your child in his pocket or backpack if he needs a reminder such as, "What I am doing after school today," if the routine has changed.

- ☐ Limit screen time to an amount you have both agreed upon ahead of time. This includes the television, phones, computers, and video games. These are a great way to escape, but can eat huge amounts of time needed for other things. Limit these things now to build good habits for the future.

- ☐ Continue to allow your child to keep a routine to his day, but encourage some occasional changes. Keeping to a routine will be something that helps him for a long time to come.

Role-Play!

Each week, help your child to go over his schedule and make sure everything is in his planner or calendar. Talk about your own schedule and the ways he will need to work his schedule around yours. Check with him at the end of each day to add any new events. Discuss priorities and which events and activities should be more important than others.

Positive Self-Talk

"I can get it all done"
"I take time out to care for myself"
"I can plan to get things done"
"I look for better ways to
get things done"
"I am relaxed"
"I have plenty of energy"

Cameron's Corner

I'm a scheduler. I figure out what I want to do and how long it takes to get it done. If I can't get something done, I fit it in another time. I don't put things off. If I have a long project, I'll start right away and do one piece at a time. I schedule which pieces I want to do and when. That way I never turn anything in late.

6

Teach Your Child The Nuances Of Communication (Communication Skills)

Don't you love the word nuance? It means a subtle difference in, or a shade of meaning, expression, or sound. It is time to begin teaching more specific rules and nuances of communication.

How?

- ☐ Teach and practice with your child the following conversational skills:
    - How to start a conversation
    - How to join a conversation
    - How to end a conversation
    - How and why to take turns in a conversation
    - How to engage in small talk
    - How to ask questions to learn more about the other person
    - How to respond verbally or nonverbally to what the other person is saying to show interest
    - How to show understanding of the other person's feelings

- ☐ Teach your child how to use "I" messages when discussing feelings with others. "I am upset," "I don't like it when…"

- ☐ Use a script from a play to practice back and forth conversation.

- ☐ Practice eye contact with your child. If she cannot maintain it, talk to her about the most important times to use it such as when talking to an adult.

- ☐ Talk about volume control and when it is appropriate to use a quiet voice, a conversational voice, and a loud outdoor voice.

- ☐ Play charades to practice nonverbal skills.

☐ Ask your child to consider joining drama at school or taking a drama class.

☐ Teach your child the following proper phone skills:
- How to make a call
- How to receive a call
- How to take a message
- How to leave a message
- What to say when the person being called is not available
- How to finish a conversation

☐ Teach levels of relationships and what is appropriate to talk about with people at each level.

Role-Play!

Practice, practice, practice, practice! Take every opportunity to engage in practice conversations with your child. Ask others to practice with her as well. When in public, have her practice her skills with people you see often such as store clerks or waiters at a restaurant. Don't judge mistakes. Instead, praise effort and reteach the skills as needed.

These are the rules:
- Those closest to the ME box are people I tell the most to.
- Box 2 with Family and Close Friends I can share personal thoughts and feelings with. I can talk to them when I need help or I am upset. I can tell them anything I am comfortable sharing.
- Box 3 has Professionals and Classmates. Kids I Know and Classmates are kids I am around all the time. I might talk to them, but they are not close friends. They might sometimes be my friend. I can talk to them about interests and stuff that happens during the day. Professional Helpers are people I might turn to for help with particular problems. I might share personal information or feelings with them according to their profession.
- Box 4 with People I see in Public are people I see often. They may know my name. I might talk to them about interests or daily events if a trusted adult is with me. I am friendly to them, but I don't tell them personal information and in most cases, I don't talk to them unless I am with an adult.
- Box 5 with Strangers are people I am polite to or in some cases people I might ignore if I don't feel safe. I **never** talk to them about personal information.

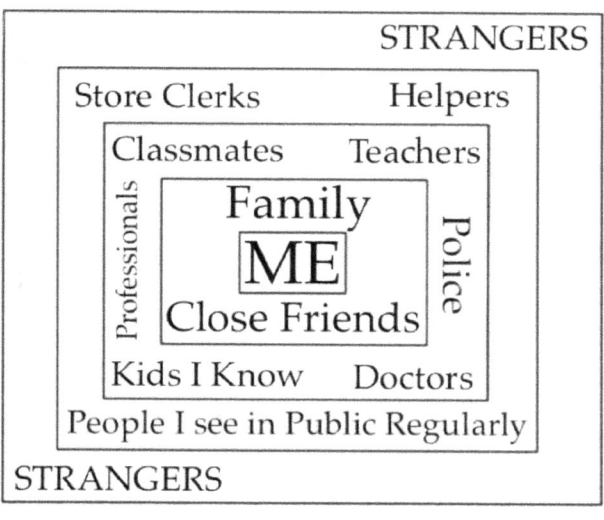

Positive Self-Talk

"I am creative"
"I am a quick thinker"
"Mistakes are great opportunities"
"I enjoy talking to others"
"I learn from those I meet"

Cameron's Corner

"I took it upon myself to practice talking to people wherever I went. If I didn't feel safe or comfortable talking to someone, I didn't. My mom also helped me know what to say in certain situations. She gave me tips to improve my conversational skills."

Special Section—Improv Games

This information is based on a book by Shawn Amador called *Teaching Social Skills Through Sketch Comedy and Improv Games: A Social Theatre ™ Approach for Kids and Teens including those with ASD, ADHD, and Anxiety.* Social Theatre is a beautiful blending of Social Stories and drama. My son credits participating in drama in high school as a major factor of his social success. He was allowed to make social mistakes with few negative consequences because it was all pretend and everyone on the stage made mistakes. He also had to learn how to project emotions through facial expressions.

Improv Games are skits specifically written to teach a social skill such as, how to enter a conversation when you come across friends who are already talking to each other. During the skit, the *main character* makes a social mistake, the characters *freeze*, and then the whole group talks about the mistake as well as a better way to handle the situation. Several social mistakes can be explored through the same skit.

Improv Games teaches social skills in a targeted way which is rarely done in schools anymore. These activities would be perfect for students of all school ages, as well as adults, and all ability levels.

Sample Improv Skit

Listen!! No Cell Phones Allowed

Characters:
Playground supervisor
Narrator
One who is talking
One who is 'listening'

Students walk together while texting
"Did you get my text?"

"Yes, I just texted you back."

Playground supervisor: "You can't have cell phones at school!" *Takes cell phones away. Walks around playground.*

Student starts talking. Other student is not listening correctly.

Other student shows ways not to listen:
1. Staring at the ceiling
2. Stare at them, but don't say anything/like a statue. No expression
3. Back towards person
4. Sarcastic excitement
5. Hands busy/wiggling

Narrator Part:
What's going on here?

What are _____'s feelings? (*point to one not being listened to*)

Yes, you are right. It made her feel bad and made her feel like she didn't want to talk to that person or maybe that that person did not like her.

Unfreeze the non-listening person: "The right way to listen is for you to look at her, nod, have a nice tone, say nice things like, "wow and cool," and ask questions!

Let's try it again!

UNFREEZE

1. The two actors engage in reciprocal conversation and listen the right way.

This skit was written by group participants of Shawn Amador and reprinted here with her permission. Please see www.socialtheatre.org for more information about Improv Games and Social Theatre™, to learn more about Amador's book, and for sample skits.

Special Section—Healing Diets

There are several healing diets, in addition to GFCF, many parents have found success with to help heal their child's digestive system, which in turn has improved the child's physical, emotional, and mental well being. Because there are so many diets, it is impossible to fully describe them here. However, please look at the resources for each diet for more information and to see if one of these diets might be right for your child.

GAPS Diet
Gut and Psychology Syndrome: Natural treatment for Autism, Dyspraxia, A.D.D., Dyslexia, A.D.H.D., Depression and Schizophrenia by Dr. Natasha Campbell-McBride
www.gapsdiet.com
("The GAPS Diet focuses on removing foods that are difficult to digest and damaging to gut flora and replacing them with nutrient-dense foods to give the intestinal lining a chance to heal and seal." Quoted from the website)

Specific Carbohydrate Diet
The SCD for Autism and ADHD: A Reference and Dairy-Free Cookbook for the Specific Carbohydrate Diet by Raman Prasad
(An elimination diet to improve the health of the digestion system)

The Wahl's Protocol
The Wahl's Protocol: A Radical New Way to Treat All Chronic Autoimmune Conditions Using Paleo Principles by Dr. Terry Wahl's

Ketogenic Diet
The Complete Ketogenic Diet for Beginners: Your Essential Guide to Living the Keto Lifestyle
 by Amy Ramos
(A diet that is very low in carbs and sugar and high in healthy fats)

Paleo Diet
Paleo for Beginners: Essentials to Get Started
by John Chatham

7

Teach Your Child To Use His Interests To Create And Meet Goals (Goal Setting)

Can you guess how many cars this young man has in his collection?

At this point, your child's interests may begin changing. Or he may still be very interested in the same things. That's okay too. Perhaps his interest in rockets will pave the way for a career one day in rocket science. Continue to encourage new things, but use his interests as a way to learn.

How?

- ☐ If your child has a large interest in a particular subject, use it to help him learn to set goals. How can he learn something new in this area? How can he achieve something or make something new?

- ☐ Consider individual or group lessons in his area of interest. This will help broaden his learning and, if in a group, to find new ways to socialize.

- ☐ Ask your child to make a list of things he would like to do or accomplish. Make it a long list filled with everything he can think of.

- ☐ Then, have him pick one or two of those things to work towards now. Show him how to create action steps for each goal. These are the steps that need to be completed in order to accomplish the goal.

- ☐ Encourage your child to start with smaller goals you know he can accomplish first. This way he will feel successful and learn the process of creating and reaching goals before moving on to bigger goals.

Book Nook

Drive—9 Ways to Motivate Your Kids to Achieve
by Janine Walker Caffrey

- ☐ Encourage some short-term (finished quickly) and some long-term goals. Encourage him to stick with the long-term goals even if he decides he might want to give up.

- ☐ If your child really wants to accomplish something, even if it seems too difficult for him, encourage him to work through the steps. Include getting help if needed as part of those steps.

- ☐ Teach your child these steps to completing a goal. Ask him to write the answers before beginning.
    1) What do you want to do?
    2) When do you plan to do it?
    3) How will you know you've done it?
    4) What are the steps to getting it done?
    5) Who can you ask for help when you need it?
    6) What is your backup plan if it doesn't work out as planned?

- ☐ Teach your child to enjoy the process, not just the outcome. If the goal doesn't turn out quite as expected he will have had fun doing the work and learning from it.

Role-Play!

Dream Big! Discuss your dreams and goals and ways you have achieved them. Let your child dream out loud about things he would like to accomplish. Don't tell him he can't do something. Let him know that anything is possible if he plans it out and works toward it. Talk about what it would take to accomplish some of his goals.

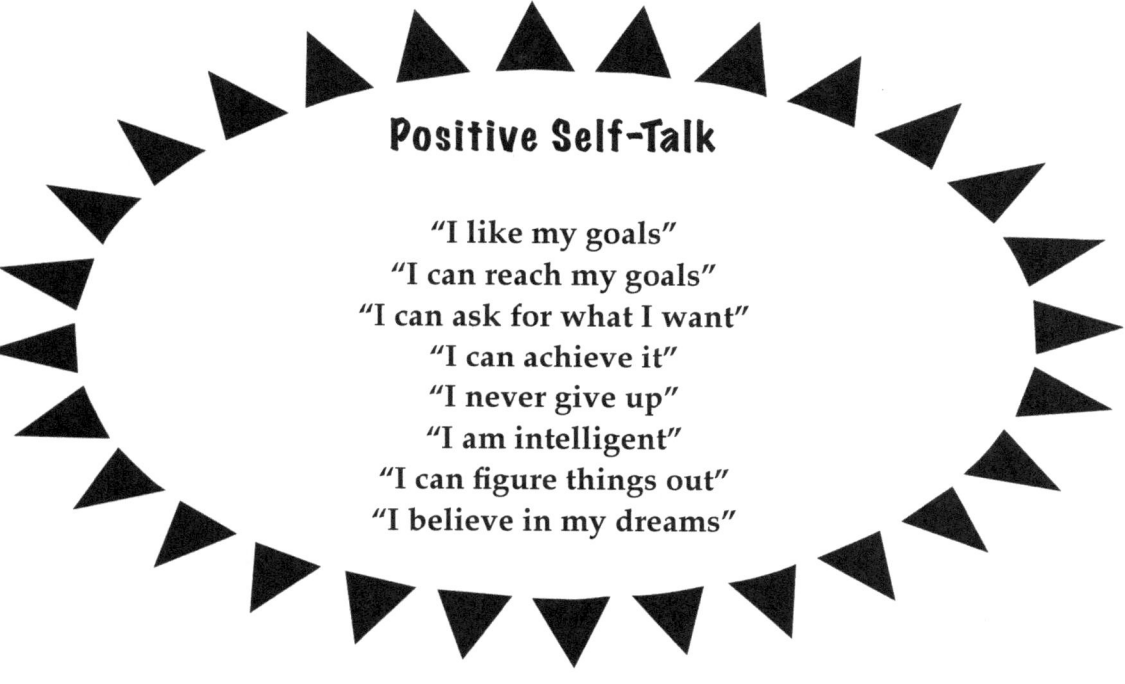

Positive Self-Talk

"I like my goals"
"I can reach my goals"
"I can ask for what I want"
"I can achieve it"
"I never give up"
"I am intelligent"
"I can figure things out"
"I believe in my dreams"

Cameron's Corner

"I have dreams and I plan my life to make sure what I do helps move me towards meeting those goals. I actively work on my goals like practicing my art, saving money, and checking my grades regularly."

8

Teach Your Child How To Step Out On Her Own (Self-Sufficiency)

Our children will not always have us with them to help them through each day. It is time to teach your child skills that will take her towards independence.

How?

- ☐ Add more responsibility to her chore list and expect her to complete the tasks without help or reminders.

- ☐ Create some learning experiences by asking your child to do things for you that you would normally do yourself such as: make a phone call, using her own cart to shop for part of the grocery list, deposit her own money at the bank, order her own food at the restaurant, take the bus to somewhere she wants to go (this is best done with a buddy, not on her own), pick out her own clothes within a budget, ride her bike to somewhere nearby she wants to go (make sure she has a cell phone for emergencies), cook a meal, plan a week's menu, or research places to go on your next vacation.

- ☐ If your child's hobbies are ones which she can make money doing, then encourage her to sell the things she creates or to perform tasks for others for pay. You may have to help and guide her to get started with this.

- ☐ Your child can learn more about herself by taking one of the well-known personality tests such as the Myers Briggs Type Indicator, Keirsey Temperament Sorter or an Enneagram test. Some of these are more complicated than others, but well worth it. When your child understands her own personality she will better understand why she does some of the things she does and the way she does them. This will also show her some difficult traits of her personality to watch out for and strive to improve.

- Teach your child that no matter how old she gets or how smart she is, she should always know when to ask for help. People who get help, when needed, live easier and less stressful lives.

- Create a support system for your child for when she needs help. This can include friends, family, church members, neighbors, teachers, mentors, doctors, counselors, and club members. Brainstorm with her the possible times she might need help, and who she would ask for help. Talk about how to keep herself safe when going to someone for help.

- Your child will probably find it difficult when others break rules. Teach her that others must deal with their own consequences and that the problems don't belong to her unless the broken rules affect her health or safety.

- Help your child learn healthy emotional boundaries by teaching her:
    1) When and how to say *no*. This includes when someone asks her to do something and she is truly too busy to put anything more on her calendar. (even if she wants to do the activity)
    2) How to keep time with her friends as equitable as possible. This means taking turns with what each wants to do for instance.
    3) To work as hard as possible to keep a positive attitude at all times.
    4) What things are not acceptable to her and what she should never put up with such as people calling her names, using her stuff and not returning it or breaking it, people wanting to come over to her house to use her video games, but never inviting her to do anything with them, using bad language, saying mean things, touching her without permission, or asking her for money or her things.

☐ Let your child make decisions for herself even when you can see a negative consequence coming. Letting her face those consequences now will teach her better decision making in the future. Be sure to give her empathy after the consequence and ask her if she would like to talk about the situation. Don't tell her, "I told you so," or lecture her. Ask her if she would like to know what she could have done differently. She may already have that answer and will not appreciate hearing it again.

Cameron's Corner

"I learned a lot through practice, practice, practice and from watching my mom do things. I also asked A LOT of questions when something didn't make sense to me."

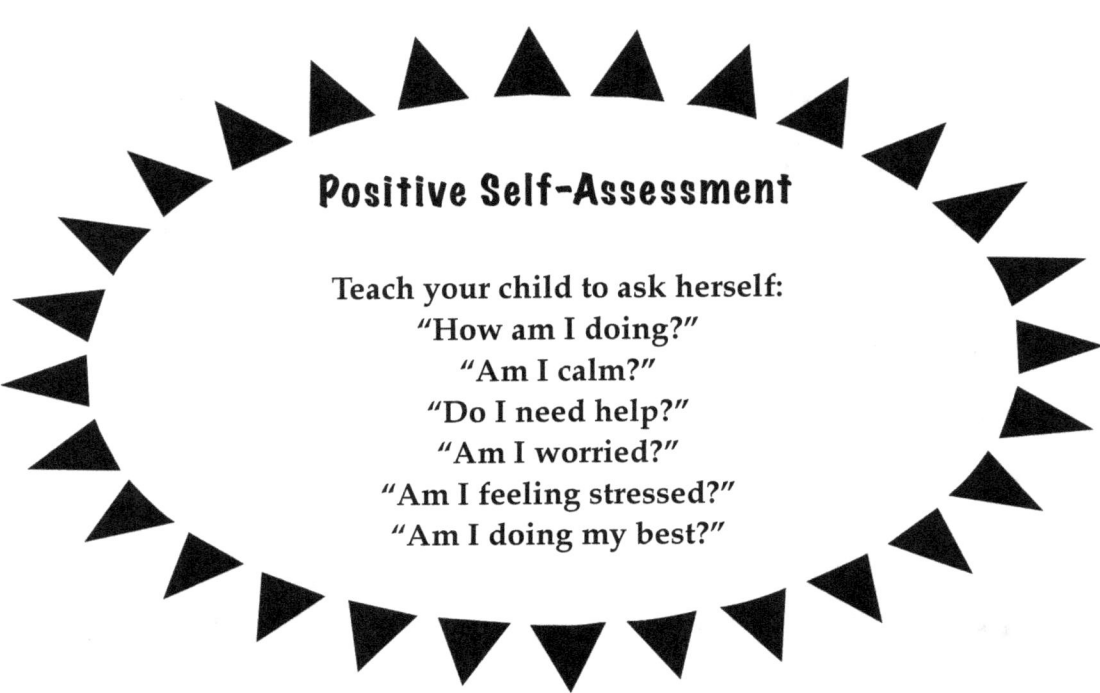

Positive Self-Assessment

Teach your child to ask herself:
"How am I doing?"
"Am I calm?"
"Do I need help?"
"Am I worried?"
"Am I feeling stressed?"
"Am I doing my best?"

Role-Play!

Model self-assessment through family meetings. Ask your child the self-assessment questions in the "you" form such as, "How are you doing?" Take interest in her answers. Ask, "What are you going to do about that?" or "How can I help you?" if she has a problem. Show her you are willing to support her as she figures things out on her own.

9

Teach Your Child How To Deal With A Build Up Of Stress And Frustration
(Stress Management)

Unfortunately, stress never goes away completely for anyone. The more your child learns to manage it now, the better he'll be able to handle it when he is on his own.

How?

Talk to your child about how stress affects the body and how to recognize the physical symptoms of stress overload. Here are some of the possible signs:

Headaches	Trouble swallowing	Nausea
Heartburn	Sweating a lot	Stomach flutters
Neck pain	Feeling tired often	Feeling dizzy
Muscle pain	Going to the bathroom often	Feeling panic
Constipation	Diarrhea	Trouble sleeping
Shaking	Fast heartbeat	Vomiting
Crying	Unexplained anger	Nail biting
Distractedness	Feeling jumpy	Sick stomach
Pain	Change in hunger	

Help your child to understand that not only can stress affect his body, but his reactions to stress can negatively affect those around him such as when he yells at someone or says something mean because he is stressed. When he does these things, point out how that made someone else feel.

Here are some more ways your child can deal with stress:
- Watch a favorite movie
- Take a warm soothing bath
- Take breaks often throughout the day
- Journaling
- Self massage (hands, feet, head)
- Acupressure on feet (roll a tennis ball under the feet)
- Footbath

- Change of routine
- Deep breathing (while in a lying or sitting position)
- Go to a quiet place and doing nothing
- Do something creative or fun
- Talk to someone
- Try doing less for a while
- Exercise
- Meditate
- Pray
- Write down a list of all the items causing stress
- When things feel out of control, talk to a counselor

Role-Play!

Each time you notice your child appears to be under more stress than usual, point it out to him. Ask him if you can help him. If he says, "No," offer ways he could help himself deal with the stress. Tell him you are concerned and want to help him feel his best.

Book Nook

Too Stressed to Think? A Teen Guide to Staying Sane When Life Makes You Crazy
by Annie Fox & Ruth Kirschner

Fighting Invisible Tigers: Stress Management for Teens
by Earl Hipp

The Feelings Book—The Care and Keeping of Your Emotions
An American Girl Book
(dealing with emotions for girls)

Cameron's Corner

"When I am stressed, I like to spend time with good friends. Having someone to talk to helps. I make sure to get plenty of rest which sometimes means going to bed early. I also find I am less stressed when I can focus my mind on something intensive like exercising."

Challenge Steps 229

Positive Self-Talk

"I can handle this"
"I am in control of my emotions"
"I can be calm"
"I can ask for what I need"
"It's okay to be upset while figuring things out"

SCHOOL

You have been working hard for your child's success at school. Now it is time for her to take on more of the responsibility of that success.

How?

- ☐ Don't agree to take your child off of her IEP until you believe she is ready. This is the teacher's guide to accommodations and will help your child during times of transitions.

- ☐ Let your child make more of the decisions regarding accommodations, classes to take, after-school activities, and so forth. Let her tell you what she can and cannot handle.

- ☐ If you feel it is appropriate, let your child be a part of the IEP meetings. Let her discuss her needs and how she feels accommodations have worked in the past.

- ☐ With each new teacher, meet to discuss your child's needs.

- ☐ If possible, at the end of the school year or before the new school year starts, meet with your child's IEP team to discuss any upcoming changes. This will help you to better prepare your child for transitions.

- ☐ Continue to ask for a person at the school to be available who your child can go to if she has questions or needs help.

- ☐ If your child has been taken off of her IEP, continue to tell each new teacher that she has ASD. This will help the teacher to better understand your child's needs. Even if she is no longer on an IEP, you can still ask the teacher for any accommodations you feel are necessary or your child asks for.

- ☐ Watch out for transitions at the beginning of each school year and each change to new classes. Help your child make the transition by going over each teacher's rules and requirements. If she begins at a new school, start over. Take your child on a tour of the school, introduce her to the new teacher(s), and walk her through the school's rules and procedures.

- ☐ If handwriting is still an issue, encourage your child to type as many of her assignments as possible.

- ☐ Check in with your child regularly and ask if her needs at school are being met.

- ☐ If you have been homeschooling, consider sending your child back to school. Some schools allow for a part-time homeschool and part-time public school situation. Check if this is an option that would work for you.

DIET

At this point, hopefully, your child is eating a nice clean diet and it is really helping, but what else can you do to make it even better?

☐ Be sure your child is getting a balanced diet. This means including plenty of fruits, vegetables, and lean protein. Remember that growing children need plenty of protein and healthy fats to grow.

What is a healthy fat?
- Uncooked Olive oil
- Nuts
- Fatty fish such as salmon and tuna
- Avocados
- Lean meats
- Seeds such as sunflower and pumpkin
- All natural peanut or other nut butters

What is an unhealthy fat?
- Most fried foods
- Trans fats found anywhere (especially margarine)
- Most mayonnaise (try Vegenaise or Nayonaise as a healthier alternative)
- Store-bought baked goods such as donuts, muffins, cookies, and cakes
- Packaged junk foods such as chips, crackers, microwave popcorn, candy bars, and most ice creams

☐ Be wary of Fat-Free or Low-Fat items. These often have a higher content of sugar or other fillers. When they take the fat away, they add something else.

- ☐ Whenever possible, make treats and snacks at home to get the best possible nutrition. Most packaged foods of this type not only have low nutritional value, but have lots of preservatives and additives.

- ☐ Make your own trail mix as a snack alternative. This can include nuts, raisins or other dried fruits, and chocolate chips without additives. Enjoy Life company makes chocolate that is dairy free, gluten free, egg free and soy free for those on a restricted allergy diet.

- ☐ Check labels on foods. You would be surprised at what manufacturers put in food. When you have a food that you eat often that is *okay*, check the labels periodically. Manufacturers change ingredients often to lower costs and to add flavor. If you can't pronounce it, don't eat it.

- ☐ Teach your family how to read food labels.

- ☐ Consider making fruit and vegetable smoothies as a way to get more nutrition in your child's diet. There are plenty of books available with smoothie recipes the whole family will enjoy.

- ☐ Explain to your child how nutrition affects his body. Tell him how good nutrition feeds and improves his body while unhealthy foods with no nutritional value harm the body.

- ☐ Above all, encourage your child to make his own healthy choices. You will not always be there to watch what he eats. Model this at home by having the best choices available. Include occasional treats in the diet. Children completely deprived of treats will find ways to get them when you are not looking. Show him how to have treats in moderation and the best choices in treats with the best nutritional value.

☐ Include probiotic and fermented foods in your diet such as low sugar yogurt (dairy free as needed), kimchi, sauerkraut, kombucha drinks (fermented tea), vegetable or fruit kvass, miso (if soy is tolerated), and fermented pickles. Fermented foods should never contain vinegar. You can search the internet for recipes and find out which brands are available where you live. GTs Kombucha and Bubbies sauerkraut and pickles are two good brands found nationally. Fermented veggies and fruits (kvass) are very easy to make at home.

Book Nook

Green Smoothie Revolution: The Radical Leap Towards Natural Health
By Victoria Boutenko

Super Food for Superchildren: Delicious, low-sugar recipes for healthy, happy children, from toddlers to teens
By Tim Noakes, Jonno Proudfoot, and Bridget Surtees

201 Healthy Smoothies & Juices for Kids
by Amy Roskelley and Nicole Cormier

Fermented Vegetables: Creative Recipes for Fermenting 64 Vegetables & Herbs in Krauts, Kimchis, Brined Pickles, Chutneys, Relishes, & Pastes
by Kirsten K Shockey and Christopher Shockey

Sweet and Savory Fat Bombs: 100 Delicious Treats for Fat Fasts, Ketogenic, Paleo, and Low-Carb Diets
by Martina Slajerova

SOCIAL TIME

There are many rules for social interaction and they can be difficult for anyone to learn. Practice advanced social skills with your child one skill at a time. Even if your child has not reached the place to begin using some of the skills, start talking about them.

- ☐ Teach her how to maintain friendships by teaching rules of friendship like:
    - Spending regular time with friends
    - Taking turns doing what each likes to do
    - Giving friends space to be with other friends or alone
    - Understanding that it is okay to have different opinions, likes, and dislikes
    - Keeping friends' personal information private
    - Keeping friends' secrets (unless safety is an issue)

- ☐ Find as many possible chances for your child to be in small group situations. Some examples are: play dates, school or community clubs, church groups, or parties.

- ☐ Explain what joking, teasing, and sarcasm are. Talk to your child about how to tell the difference between when these things are friendly and when they are not.

- ☐ Teach your child how to have a good attitude when winning or losing. Model this behavior.

- ☐ If your child has a friendship that you find negative or difficult, don't jump in to terminate that relationship or give advice. If the child is enjoying the relationship, be supportive. Reflect her feelings when things go badly, "I see you are frustrated that Lucy often breaks your toys. What are you going to do about it?" If the relationship poses a risk to safety or causes severe emotional harm, you should jump in. Otherwise, give your child a chance to figure things out on her own.

- ☐ Encourage your child to volunteer as often as possible.

- ☐ Encourage your child to join school groups such as band, orchestra, drama, choir, or clubs as she is interested.

- ☐ Teach about kindness which shows friendliness, caring, and concern. Talk about times kindness helps others and ways to show it. Model this behavior.

- ☐ Teach about empathy which is the understanding and sharing of feelings. Talk about times people may need empathy and how this can help.

- ☐ Even though it is exciting to have your child socializing and making friends, set limits to how much time she can spend away from home and in activities.

- ☐ As your child enters her mid-teenage years, discuss rules of dating. Go over these rules one step at a time so she understands all the dos and don'ts.

Book Nook

The Unwritten Rules of Friendship: Simple Strategies to Help Your Child Make Friends
by Natalie M. Elman & Eileen Kennedy-Moore

EXERCISE

If your child is ready, it is time to challenge his body with more invigorating exercise. This will help him build strength and stamina.

How?

- ☐ Your child should be maintaining daily exercise of at least 30 minutes. Change up the routine with different forms of exercise. On rainy or cold days, exercise indoors.

- ☐ Put your child on a sports team. Choose a sport he enjoys the most. Think outside of the box when choosing a sport such as a swim team, golf team, gymnastics, or horseback riding. Find a team that is not highly competitive. If your child's strengths are not athletics, keep your expectations low. Tell him he is there to have fun and to meet new people. Excelling and winning should not be at the top of the priority list. If your child absolutely does not want to play sports, do not force him.

- ☐ Continue regular balance activities. Consider DVDs for balance ball exercises or Tai Chi for indoor activity.

- ☐ Find some indoor exercise routines your child likes. Include light weights.

- ☐ Ask your child to help with the heavy outdoor chores such as washing the car, raking leaves, or weeding the garden.

- ☐ Try some of the following activities:
    - Bike to somewhere away from home

- Rollerblading
- Tennis
- Archery
- Nature walk
- Swimming

☐ If you are a family who loves the outdoors try:
- Camping
- Water rafting
- Canoeing/Kayaking
- Rock climbing (this can be done indoors)
- A Water park
- Waterskiing
- Snow skiing
- Boating
- Fishing
- Hiking

Special Section—Where Do We Go From Here?

Even once you have reached a place where things are manageable, continue to evaluate your child's needs and fine-tune everything.

Keep the lines of communication open. Constantly talk together about how things are going. Be supportive and continue to help your child to find answers.

Even though Cameron is completely independent, there are still issues that crop up from time to time. Sometimes there are things he doesn't know how to do, or other times he simply needs reassurance that the way he is doing something is correct.

If there is one thing I would like every parent to take away from this book, it is this: Never give up hope and never stop learning and teaching. Fix your eyes on the goals you have set for yourself and your child, do everything possible to reach them, and step by step you will find success.

Book Nook

Topics for Teens and Adults with ASD

Asperger Syndrome at Work
DVD by Coulter Video

Growing Up on the Spectrum—A Guide to Life, Love and Learning for Teens and Young Adults with Autism and Asperger's
by Lynn Kern Koegel and Claire LaZebnik
(A guide for parents and teens who want more information beyond the basics)

22 Things a Woman With Asperger's Syndrome Wants Her Partner to Know
by Rudy Simone

22 Things a Woman Must Know If She Loves a Man with Asperger's Syndrome
by Rudy Simone

How to Get a Date Worth Keeping: Be Dating in Six Months or Your Money Back
by Henry Cloud
(a guide to dating)

Boundaries in Dating: How Healthy Choices Grow Healthy Relationships
by Henry Cloud and John Townsend

Special Section—Where Did We Begin?

(Cameron's Story)

As a little kid, I had few to no friends. I had a hard time connecting with others. As I grew and matured, I learned to be social even though it was hard with Asperger's. When I entered middle school, I had the capability of making friends, but I was still unsure how to socially keep friendships going.

Even as a young child I was interested in music and art. Throughout middle school, I was in band playing drums. I loved creating art especially all kinds of portraits. Over the years I have won dozens of competitions for my creations and photography as well. Also, recently I made it in to varsity choir, chasing my love of singing.

There is another kind of art I do which is theater. I've always been interested in acting and performing. My love of singing goes hand in hand with musicals. I even managed to land the leading role in Romeo and Juliet my freshman year of high school. I plan to go to college and get a degree in interdisciplinary art.

Traversing high school, I have managed to make long-lasting friendships on my own. In present day, I crave friendship and will one day want the one person I will live with the rest of my life.

Update: As of today, Cameron has graduated from a four-year university with a bachelor's degree in interdisciplinary art. He worked full time the entire four years he was in school. He now plans to work as an electrical engineer while painting in his spare time. Next month, he will be moving out to live on his own with a roommate.

An award-winning drawing by Cameron O'Hair from middle school

A Mothers' Note

I am proud of my son. Cameron ignored the doubters and has come miles and miles from where he began. He still has a few miles to go, but I know he will travel those as well, because he too believes in achieving his goals, no matter the odds.

ABA, 50, 174
Advocates, 74
Allergies, food, 78, 185
Amino acids, 187
Aromatherapy, 198
ASD, how to explain, 10
Asperger's, 5
Attitude, 126
Autism Spectrum Disorder, traits of, 5
Balance, 122, 164
Bed time routine, 34, 70
Bedding, 27
Bedroom,
    cleaning, 35, 199
    furnishing, 28
    light, 28
Behavior, 174
Biomedical interventions, 185
Blame, 5
Blanket, weighted, 29, 69, 71
Body Language,
    eye contact, 29, 39, 133, 207
    facial expressions, 109
    learning, 132
    personal space, 82
Body safety, 63
Boundaries,
    healthy, 220
    personal, 82
Breathing exercise, 84
Bullies, 115
Caffeine, 159
Candida albicans, 186

Change, 33, 137, 193
Chelation therapy, 187
Choices, 49, 142
Chores, 52, 144
Clothing, discomfort, 27
Clubs, 233
Collections, 45
Comfy place, 18
Communication, 38, 131, 206
Creative language, 40, 132
Cures, 7, 89
Dairy free diet, 79
Decision making, 189
Diagnosis, 5
Diet, 78, 158, 230
    GAPS, 213
    Healing, 213
Digestive enzymes, 186
DIRFloortime, 100
Eating, picky, 28
Emotions, 110
Exercise, 83, 164, 235
Eye contact, 29, 39, 133, 207
Family meetings, 146
Five Point Scale, 148
Flexibility, 193
GAPS diet, 213
Girls with ASD, 67
Gluten free diet, 79
Goal setting, 214
Group play, 233
Help, finding, 74, 155
Hugging, 27

"I" messages, 207
Idioms, 132
IEP (Individual Education Plan), 72-76
Improve Games, 211
Independence, 218
Interests and hobbies, 45
Internet safety, 117
Language, creative, 40. 132
Law, teaching, 115
Love & Logic (Cline & Fay), 49, 142
Manners, 163
Medication, for sleep, 71
Meltdowns, 55
Mentors, 90
Mistakes, 191
Motor skills, 83
Multivitamin, 78
Narrating, 41, 102, 133
Nonverbal children, 153
Nutrition, 78, 158, 230
Obsessions, 45
Omega-3 oils, 158
PDD (Pervasive Development Disorder), 5
PEC (Picture Exchange System), 153
Peer pressure, 65
Play,
    dates, 81
    therapy, 100
Positive thinking, 126

Probiotics, 158
Problem solving, 189
Processed foods, 78, 158
Propioception, 123
Routines,
    bedtime, 34, 70
    daily, 34
    departure, 34
    evening, 29, 34
    morning, 29, 34
    school, 37
Rules, teaching, 22
Safe Zones, 67
Safety, 63, 115
Safety,
    body, 63
    internet, 117
    social media, 116
Scaffolding, 135
Schedule,
    daily, 34
    family, 33
    school, 37
School, 72, 156, 228
School, accommodations, 72, 156
Self-esteem, 180
Self-assessment, 219
Self-regulation, 123
Sensory Bags, 67

Sensory, integration, 118
Sensory activities,
    auditory, 122
    balance, 122
    oral, 121
    proprioception, 123
    self-regulation, 123
    smell, 121
    touch, 121
    visual, 122
Sensory issues, 26
    at school, 31
    in public, 30
    light, 28
    smells, 28
    touch, 27
Siblings, 12
Sign language, 153
Single parents, 155
Sleep,
    medication, 71
    problems, 70
    sensory issues, 70
    strategies, 70
Social,
    rules, 22
    skills, 81, 160, 233
    stories, 106
Social media safety, 116
Social Theatre, 211
Sports, 84, 235
Stimming, 43

Stranger danger, 63
Stress, 147, 223
Stress management, 223
Sugar, avoiding, 78, 158
Support groups, 89
Tantrums, 55
Therapy,
    aquatic, 172
    animal assisted, 172
    auditory integration, 169
    behavior, 174
    light, 173
    massage, 174-6
    movement, 172
    music, 171
    neurofeedback, 170
    occupational, 168
    physical, 168
    play, 100
    sensory integration, 169
    speech, 171
    vision, 169
Time management, 203
Touch, 27
Travel bag, 20
Treatment, individualized, 5
Treatment plan, 89
Vitamin and mineral testing, 186
Volunteering, 182
Yoga Ball, 68
Weighted blanket, 29, 69, 71

Acknowledgements

Thank you to Melanie Brown and Rainbow and Garon Tornell for your contributions and support. Thank you, Susan D'Avanzo, for sparking an idea.

Thank you, Gwen O'Hair, for your support in every way imaginable.

Thank you to Shawn Amador for the use of your improv skit.

Thank you to Silke Stein for creating an amazing cover. You can find her at www.bookcovergirl.jimdo.com.

Thank you to author Jenny-Lee for your amazing insights and tips, for helping clean up after the gremlins, and for believing in the possibility of epic!

About The Author

Emmaline MacBeath is a former educator who has worked with children of all ages for over 20 years. She holds a master of education as well as a master of business management. When she isn't writing fiction for children and young adults, under the pen name, Emmaline Rose, as well as nonfiction books, Emmaline solves family mysteries as a genetic genealogist.

She lives in the Pacific Northwest and is the very proud mom of two sons.

You can find her at www.emmalinerosebooks.com

Cameron O'Hair is Emmaline's adult son. He graduated this week from university with a BA in Interdisciplinary Art. Although he was born with Asperger's, he has overcome it. He has gained many social circles and loves to hang out. Cameron creates art in many forms including drawing, painting, theater, photography, and music.

Ryan Winters is Emmaline's adult son. He has been drawing in some form since he could hold sidewalk chalk and crayons. In sixth grade, he began drawing in the manga style and he continues to progress while developing his own style. He will soon be attending college to complete two art programs.

One of the greatest gifts you can give to an author is to leave feedback wherever you purchased this paperback or ebook. Thank you!

www.ingramcontent.com/pod-product-compliance
Lightning Source LLC
Chambersburg PA
CBHW051402070526
44584CB00023B/3264